SEAN O'CASEY'S

DRAMA

To Georgia

SEAN O'CASEY'S DRAMA

VERISIMILITUDE AND VISION

Ronald Gene Rollins

THE UNIVERSITY OF ALABAMA PRESS
University, Alabama

ACKNOWLEDGMENTS

I am grateful to the following publishers and agents for permission to quote from books which they have purchased or control:
To New Books Publications for passages from *Fiery Cross: the Story of Jim Larkin*(1963) by Joseph Deasy. To Aurora Publishers, Inc. and Macmillan & Co. Ltd. for passages from *Sean O'Casey: Modern Judgements*(1970) ed. Ronald Ayling. To Columbia University Press and *The Review of Religion* for passages from "The Dying God in the Modern Theatre," (March, 1941) by Winifred Smith. To the Oxford University Press for passages from *The Achievement of T. S. Eliot*(1935) by F. O. Matthiessen. To St Martin's Press, Inc. for passages from *Blasts and Benedictions*(1967) selected by Ronald Ayling; *Under a Colored Cap*(1963) by Sean O'Casey; *The Sean O'Casey Reader* (1968) ed. Brooks Atkinson; and *The Experiments of Sean O'Casey*(1960) by Robert Hogan. To St Martin's Press, Inc. and Macmillan & Co. of New York and London for passages from *Three Plays*(1960) by Sean O'Casey; *Collected Plays*, Vols. II-III-IV(1964, 1967, 1958) by Sean O'Casey; and *Mirror in My House*, Vols. I-II(1956) by Sean O'Casey. To M. B. Yeats, Miss Anne Yeats, Macmillan & Co., Ltd. and A. P. Watt & Son for passages from *Essays and Introductions*(1961) by W. B. Yeats; and *The Letters of W. B. Yeats*(1954) ed. Allan Wade. To Trinity College, Cambridge, and Macmillan & Co., Ltd. for passages from *The Golden Bough*(1940) by Sir James G. Frazer. To the Lady Gregory Estate and Colin Smythe Ltd. for passages from *Lady Gregory's Journals, 1916–1930*(1946) ed. Lennox Robinson. To Routledge & Kegan Paul Ltd. for passages from *The Poet in the Theatre*(1946) by Ronald Peacock. To Harcourt Brace Jovanovich, Inc./Farrar, Straus & Giroux, Inc. for passages from *Selected Prose of T. S. Eliot*(1975) ed. Frank Kermode. To The Society of Authors for the Bernard Shaw Estate for passages from *Selected Plays with Prefaces*, Vol. II(1949) by Bernard Shaw. To Anthony Sheil Associates Ltd. for passages from *The Face and Mind of Ireland*(1950) by Arland Ushher. To the Devin-Adair Company for passages from *1000 Years of Irish Prose*(1952) ed. Vivian Mercier and David H. Greene; *1000 Years of Irish Poetry*(1947) ed. Kathleen Hoagland; and *Three Great Irishmen: Shaw, Yeats, Joyce* (1957) by Arland Ussher. To Doubleday & Co., Inc. for passages from *Comedy*(1956) intro. Wylie Sypher. To George Braziller, Inc. for passages from *The Green Crow*(1956) by Sean O'Casey. To the Macmillan Co., Ltd. and the New American Library for passages from *The Genius of the Irish Theatre* (1960) eds. Sylvan Barnet, Morton Berman, and William Burto. To Dodd, Mead & Company for passages from *Drama: The Major Genres* (1962) by Robert Hogan and Sven Eric Molin. To *The New York Times* and Eileen O'Casey for passages "From 'Within the Gates'," (October 21, 1934) by Sean O'Casey. To the University of Toronto and *Modern Drama* for passages from "The Sources and Themes of *The Plough and the Stars*" (December, 1961) by W. A. Armstrong; "Sean O'Casey and the Road to Expressionism" (December, 1961) by Vincent C. De Baun; "Sean O'Casey and Expressionism" (May, 1970) by Joan Templeton.—Ronald G. Rollins, Ohio 1977

Library of Congress Cataloging in Publication Data

Rollins, Ronald Gene.
Sean O'Casey's drama.

Bibliography: p.
Includes index.
1. O'Casey, Sean, 1880–1964—Criticism and interpretation. I. Title.
PR6029.C33Z79 1978b 822'.9'12 77-14462
ISBN 0-8173-7327-6

Manufactured in the United States of America

CONTENTS

Preface vii

1. Profile of a People and a Playwright: Verisimilitude and Vision 1
2. Ireland in a State of "Chassis": The Dublin Trilogy 12
3. Dramas of Ceremonial Ritualism and Symbolic Stylization 41
4. Aristophanic Allegories: Myth and Magic 78
5. O'Casey Confesses and Comments: A Look at His Letters 100

Appendix 113
Notes 130
Bibliography 137
Index 138

PREFACE

This brief book will, it is hoped, provide some insights into Sean O'Casey, the man and artist, and into the seminal aspects of selected, representative plays from the early, middle, and late phases of his career. After a suggestive prelude, which argues that the Irish in general (and O'Casey in particular) are people with two faces, one poetic and the other pragmatic, I move to *The Plough and the Stars*, O'Casey's early masterpiece, which shows him using a cinematographic technique as visual impressions succeed and overlap each other, and a formula of alternating concentration and expansion as passages of low intensity set off major dramatic moments. I move next through three plays of his middle period, *The Silver Tassie*, *Within the Gates*, and *Purple Dust*, noting especially O'Casey's increasing use of ritualistic, ceremonial patterns of conduct and symbolic, surrealistic landscapes. O'Casey's management and marriage of myths is a major concern of the fourth chapter, which studies *Cock-a-Doodle Dandy* and *The Drums of Father Ned*, two fantasies that present diametrically opposite views of Ireland. In my discussion of these six plays, I emphasize the recurrent contrast of verisimilitude and vision.

When appropriate, I have inserted in the text quotations from O'Casey's letters. In the interest of readability, these quotations have been silently amended. In chapter 5 I have commented upon the remaining O'Casey letters to me. Facsimiles of all the letters are collected in an appendix at the end of the book.

Portions of this book have appeared in the *Irish University Review*, *Éire-Ireland*, *The Explicator*, *Philological Papers*, *The Shaw Review*, *Modern Drama*, and the *James Joyce Quarterly*. However, significant revisions, involving deletions and expansions, have been made in a number of passages.

I wish to thank Eileen O'Casey, the late Dr. William Smith Clark of the University of Cincinnati, Professors A. M. Tyson and Eric Thorn of Marshall University, and my associate,

David Osborne, of Ohio Wesleyan University, for their assistance in preparing the book. My indebtedness to David Krause, Robert Hogan, and Ronald Ayling, distinguished O'Casey scholars, is apparent.

If the book enables O'Casey readers further to comprehend and appreciate O'Casey's artistry, I shall not have labored in vain.

Delaware, Ohio 1977 RONALD GENE ROLLINS

SEAN O'CASEY'S

DRAMA

ONE

PROFILE OF A PEOPLE AND A PLAYWRIGHT: VERISIMILITUDE AND VISION

We're a tormented people. There are the Irish who say little because they're afraid to say anything: these torment themselves; there's the Irish who shout out everything they have to say, indifferent to a blessing, unafraid of a curse: these are tormented by others. Oh, how mighty we'd be if it wasn't for the disturbers! They're always somewhere. However silent the world may become, there's always an Irishman somewhere bawling out an opinion in play, poem, or speech, embarrassing many, and raising a cry of woe.—O'Casey, *The Green Crow*

Arland Ussher concludes his provocative *The Face and Mind of Ireland* (1950), an impressionistic evaluation of various idioms, interludes, ideologies, and idiosyncrasies in relatively recent Irish history, by boldly presenting a diagnosis of the Irish temperament, which alternately dictates drastically different responses to reality:

> The Irishman, as I see him, is something of a realist and something of a mystic. In his literature he wavers continually between fantasy and farcicality; his most successful *genre*—from the Cuchulainn epic to *Ulysses*—is a sort of surrealistic extravaganza which has no precise parallel elsewhere. . . . Like Swift, he feels vividly that Matter is dirt and that Man is an unclean, irreclaimable, animal. . . . On the other hand, like Berkeley, he knows that this material world is a trick, unwearyingly repeated, of that very old-Gaelic magician the light, and that truth must be both nearer and farther from us than the sun.

> Man as knowing Subject is a God—as the Object who is known he is the Yahoo. . . . They are, of course, extreme and inhuman truths, inappropriate perhaps—if held in this intensity—for ordinary striving men; in combination they produce the Irishman's temperament of an almost priest-like mildness, varying with explosions of startling, apparently causeless, fury.[1]

This analysis of the Irish temperament as an admixture of different, antithetical inclinations is reiterated by Arland Ussher in his *Three Great Irishmen* (1957), a brief but insightful book providing occasional glimpses into the genius of Shaw, Yeats, and Joyce:

> The Irishman—like the Spaniard—has both a peasant shrewdness and a tendency to unworldly dreaming; the Irishman who stays in Ireland becomes a petty huckster or a whiskey-sodden poet, but the Irish emigrant—the 'wild goose' of tradition—is capable of becoming a *conquistador*. The soft Irish earth is a bog for the feet of the weak, but can be the best of springboards for the strong; and the Irish mist, which so easily turns foothills into mountains, can lure and challenge as well as 'damp' and depress.[2]

George Bernard Shaw's conjectures about the character of his countrymen synchronize with and support Ussher's, as *John Bull's Other Island* (1904), Shaw's major contribution to the Irish Renaissance, reveals. In the segments of the preface devoted to answering the question "What is an Irishman?" Shaw observes: "Our delicacy is part of a keen sense of reality which makes us a very practical, and even, on occasion, a very coarse people."[3] Later he adds that the Irishman has "a power of appreciating art and sentiment without being duped by them into mistaking romantic figments for realities."[4] In short, Shaw conceives of the representative Irishman as a person with "one eye always on things as they are."[5]

Reversing the traditional, stereotyped images of the Irishman as the romantic sentimentalist and the Englishman as a conservative rationalist, and insisting that it is part of the superiority of the Irish to dislike and mistrust fools, Shaw declares that when he sees:

> Irishmen everywhere standing clearheaded, sane, hardily callous to the boyish sentimentalities, susceptibilities, and credulities that make the Englishman the dupe of every charlatan and the idolater of every numskull, I perceive that Ireland is the only spot on earth which still produces the ideal Englishman of history. Blackguard, bully, drunkard, liar, foulmouth, flatterer . . . all these your Irishman may easily be . . . but he is never quite the hysterical, nonsense-crammed, fact-proof, truth-terrified, unballasted sport of all the bogey panics and all the silly enthusiasms that now calls itself 'God's Englishman.' England cannot do without its Irish . . . because it cannot do without at least a little sanity.[6]

Yet Shaw was perspicacious enough to realize that the Irishman had another "eye," an eye that habitually strained itself in an effort to catch glimpses of the unearthly, the mysterious, and the supernatural—of Kathleen ni Houlihan, Cuchulain, the ancient Fenian warriors, Angus, and angels—or to recreate the splendor of a Christian heaven or the inviting Arcadian landscape of Ireland's heroic past. This was the Irishman's poetic eye, which sought to transform or transcend the mundane.

Sagacious Shaw knew that the Irishman, with his imagination that initiated frequent, long interludes of "torturing, heart-scalding, never satisfying dreaming, dreaming, dreaming, dreaming,"[7] repeatedly recoiled from the ugly and abrasive aspects of his daily life, retreating into drink or dream where life, grotesque or glorious, might be commensurate with his private but intense aspirations. Lawrence Doyle, a romantic realist who resembles Shaw himself, explains how the Irishman's imagination compels him to reject the imperfect real in quest of a nebulous, more satisfying ideal, in this long speech from *John Bull's Other Island:*

> An Irishman's imagination never lets him alone, never convinces him, never satisfies him; but it makes him that he cant face reality nor handle it nor conquer it: he can only sneer at them that do. . . . Its all dreaming, all imagination. He cant be religious. The inspired Churchman that teaches him the sanctity of life and the importance of conduct is sent away empty; while the poor village priest that gives him a miracle or a sentimental story of a saint has cathedrals built for him out of the pennies of the poor. He cant be intelligently political: he dreams of what the Shan Van Vocht said in ninetyeight. If you want to interest him in Ireland youve got to call the unfortunate island Kathleen ni Hoolihan and pretend shes a little old woman. It saves thinking. It saves working. It saves everything except imagination, imagination, imagination; and imagination's such a torture than you cant bear it without whiskey. . . . At last you get that you can bear nothing real at all: youd rather starve than cook a meal; youd rather go shabby and dirty than set your mind to take care of your clothes and wash yourself; you nag and squabble at home because your wife isnt an angel, and she despises you because youre not a hero; and you hate the whole lot round you because theyre only poor slovenly useless devils like yourself.[8]

Hence Ussher and Shaw detect and define a dichotomy—a discernible duality—in this hypothetical, often tormented Irishman. They agree that the Irish, like most men, are alternately pragmatic or poetic, possessing polarized proclivities that propel them first in one direction, then in another. When in a Sancho Panza mood, the Irishman can function in a Joycean Dublin of penury, patriotism, and prostitution, a debris-littered city of monotony and mind-forged manacles. He can, for example, work during the week, purchase food and fuel, and make it to confession, intermittently complaining of the power of the priests and the imperialism of the English. Yet to counterbalance this life of monotonous regularity he must, at intervals, escape into drink or dream, momentarily discarding his daily concerns to brood, perhaps, about the splendor and permanence of a city like Yeats' Byzantium. This is the Irishman's Don Quixote mood, a hopeful, idealistic attitude that is critical of—indeed, irritated with—visible, concrete phenomena—the imperfect real. From Dublin drabness to Byzantine brilliance—this movement might symbolically summarize much of the Irishman's fluctuation.

Sean O'Casey, Irish dramatist, resembles the emblematic Irishman vivisected by Ussher and Shaw as he is a pragmatist and a poet—a realist fond of reverie—with a "keen sense of reality" and an inordinate fondness for "unworldly dreaming." O'Casey's early experiences in a harsh and difficult Dublin milieu compelled him to confront an ugly and fragmented reality, and trained him in the art of survival in a decaying, disease-pervaded slum world where concern for shelter, food, and employment were part of the continuing crisis.

Commenting upon the widespread degradation of the laboring class by the social and economic servitude of Dublin during the early years of the twentieth century, Joseph Deasy writes:

> The poverty of the labouring classes in Dublin was appalling. The city had one of the highest death rates in Europe, 27.6 per 1,000, as high, in fact, as India's Calcutta. Her slums were the worst in the United Kingdom. There were approximately 5,322 tenement houses in the city in which 'lived' 25,822 families. . . . 20,108 families occupied one room, 4,402 of the remainder had two rooms each. . . . If Dublin slum figures were higher than in the rest of the U.K., her wage rates were lower. The average wage for an adult male worker was approximately 18/- per week (equal now to £5 approx) but thousands laboured for 14/- to 16/- for a 70 hour week, while women's wages were as low as 5/-. Rents were higher than in Britain.[9]

Forced in 1894 to seek employment at age fourteen, O'Casey worked for several years as a stock boy, clerk, and railway worker, eventually aligning himself with the Irish Transport and General Worker's Union and Jim Larkin, a labor organizer with the zeal and courage of a Biblical prophet.[10] Involvement with Larkin and Irish labor at Liberty Hall from 1909 to 1914 intensified O'Casey's class consciousness and his hatred of the demonic trinity of disorder, disease, and death. His savage *indignatio* surfaces in this passage from his autobiography:

> Frequently, he wandered, hurt with anger, through these cancerous streets that were incensed into resigned woe by the rotting houses, a desperate and dying humanity, garbage and shit in the roadway; where all the worst diseases were the only nobility present; where the ruddy pictures of the Sacred Heart faded into a dead dullness by the slimy damp of the walls oozing through them. . . . Many times, as he wandered there, the tears of rage would flow into his eyes, and thoughts of bitter astonishment made him wonder why the poor worm-eaten souls there couldn't rise in furious activity, and tear the guts out of those who kept them as they were.[11]

Yet O'Casey was never content to concentrate exclusively upon the problems confronting Irish labor and its Irish Citizen Army, or the Irish Republican Army with its cadre of zealots and potential martyrs, organizations committed to drastic utilitarian or revolutionary actions that would alleviate the abrasive economic and political ills in Ireland. He must, at infrequent moments of leisure and meditation, turn away from the maelstrom of Dublin—a Dublin swarming with patriots, paudeens, and priests—and seek aesthetic pleasure and spiritual delight from another source. He must lift his glance from drab Dublin to gaze toward shining Byzantium (or its symbolic equivalent) because, like William Butler Yeats, another sensitive Irishman with weak eyes, he was addicted to reverie,[12] to what Shaw alluded to as long sessions of "scalding" dreaming. O'Casey indicates that, as a frightened and frail schoolboy with bandaged eyes, he occasionally escaped the demanding and at times painful confines of the classroom by retreating into reverie. In this passage he traces his transition from the onerous world of books and a cruel schoolmaster into an imaginary but bountiful landscape—the Kingdom of Heaven—not unlike William Blake's green and pleasant place:

> The master led him over to a class that was droning out tables, and sat him down on a bench between two boys, telling him to be good, keep his eye on the teacher. . . . Johnny's one eye glanced dreamily at the green, brown, yellow, and purple countries on a map of the world . . . as all the children of the whole wide world murmured four 'n five are nine . . . going along a . . . road white as the driven snow. . . . Then Johnny was led away to a bath, hidden in blooming hawthorn, in which the water was lovely and hot and fully perfumed. When he had been bathed, he was . . . then . . . dressed in silks. Then he was declared to be fit and free to wander about . . . over hill, meadow, and dale. . . . Suddenly . . . his hand was torn by a bitter pain. . . . He shoved the bandage from his good eye, and saw the whitish eyes of the schoolmaster staring down at him. Is this the place for sleep?[13]

At another time he attempts to escape the pain in his eyes and the depressing awareness of his ragged clothes by riding his celestial omnibus into an active world of brave men engaged in heroic warfare:

> He thickened the folds of his bandage and covered his eyes again so that the light in the room became a deep darkness. He stayed still, breathing softly, creeping close to sleep, connecting his thoughts with a world of marching troops; the clatter of guns rollin' over the stony sthreet; the jingle of cavalry swords hangin' by the hips of the riders. . . . All the people cheered an' cheered, as the Fermanaghs surged forward at a gallop, heads sthrainin' to the front, shoulders gathered together. . . . The sham battle came on, and off the Army went into hidlins; with the cavalry an' mosta the infanthry goin' one way, an' the Fermanagh Fusiliers an' Grahams goin' another.[14]

This habit of indulging in reverie—imaginative gymnastics or wish projection—persisted as O'Casey moved into manhood. Sometimes his periods of relaxation in the evening became extended sessions of imaginative exercise. In one instance, after fifteen hours of exhausting toil, O'Casey, reciting aloud passages from Shakespeare and Goldsmith, walks to his window to scrutinize Dublin in the darkness; he subsequently conjures up, in Joycean fashion, the ancient Danes who fought to extend their dominion over Ireland:

> He paused at the window, and looked out on the naked night. . . . Over beyond the canal towered the ugly bloated spire of the Catholic church, a tapering finger on a fat hand beckoning to the ships that came sailing into the Bay of Dublin. . . . All round where Johnny was looking, ah, many, many years ago, the Danes and the Irish grappled together in their last fierce fight. . . . Here the black-browed Thor went down before the gentle, golden-headed Jesus. . . . The Danish Dubliners watched from their Woden walls the armies hacking and slashing and slaying and thrusting each other. . . . He must stop his dusky dreaming, and go back to the glow of his work.[15]

It is apparent, therefore, that O'Casey does resemble the hypothetical Irishman delineated by Ussher and Shaw because he is a man with two faces, with two distinct temperamental aspects. As a former pick-and-shovel laborer and a refugee from a Dublin slum world of bondage and blight, O'Casey manifests the tenacity, shrewdness, courage, candor, wage-consciousness, practicality, and sardonic sense of humor, all coupled with an irreverence for the powerful and the pretentious, that are an inevitable part of the legacy of those who have lived too long amidst pain and privation. Yet as a sensitive and imaginative Irish dreamer O'Casey is very much the Blakean hope-fostered visionary, an inspired poet-prophet who is continually contrasting, in his utopian projections, this present world of hunger and hurt with an indistinct but realizable future world of beauty and blessedness. Thus it is this poetic impulse in O'Casey that enables him to transcend his disappointment with mundane matters and enables him "to resist the duties of life, the threat of death, and relax in loud hilarity as if the sun himself were a dancer, sorrow and pain merely mists on a mirror."[16]

When confronted with this diagnosis—this sympathetic "dissection"—which argued that he was a gifted and restless Irishman with two faces, O'Casey responded to me as follows:

> I glanced at your venture into the spacious area of O'Casey's promptings appearing in his plays; but I didnt try to read them for two reasons: first because I have to limit my reading (Eye-Doctor's orders); and, secondly because I never read, or rarely read, except when published, any opinions or thoughts that make comments upon what I have tried to do.
>
> I get reams of these MSS asking me to comment, and were I to do so, my time would be up, my eyes gone, my heart broken.
>
> My dear Ronald, I have more than Two faces! I have many; but, by and large, I think you are right insofar that the two chief ones are realistic and lyrical (I hope).
>
> Peter Balashov of the Gorki Academy of Science and the Arts, Moscow, in an article in a Soviet Magazine, says the same thing as you, comparing me to a well-known Soviet Asian poet; and a letter from Anne Elistratova, Union of Soviet Writers, who has just had a book published in the USSR on the Romantic Poets of England, [reveals] that my biography reminds her of Byron's CHILDE HAROLD. (See Appendix, p. 122.)

An awareness of this duality—this psychic ambivalence—in O'Casey's person may enable one to comprehend more completely his dramas, especially the recurrent contrast of verisimilitude and vision that is present in virtually all of them. Perhaps it is not unreasonable to suggest that the realist-dreamer syndrome in the playwright is responsible, to some extent, for the verisimilitude-vision counterpoint—for the contrast between what is and what might be—in his plays. Certainly the realistic particulars (circumstantial evidence) are presented in a manner reminiscent of journalist-novelist Daniel Defoe in the three Dublin plays, as we move through the grimy, cluttered rooms in the battered tenements of those trapped in these hovels of despair and debate. Certainly, O'Casey is anxious, as playwright-proletarian, to focus attention upon the hostility and humiliation attendant upon such ghetto existence, be it in Ireland or elsewhere.

The concern with verisimilitude—with the arrangement of the recognizably "real" particulars of locale and dress—drops sharply in the plays which immediately follow the Dublin trilogy. We get only selected symbolic variables as O'Casey, while not ignoring the religious bigotry and hypocrisy or the economic inequality in the present, begins intermittently to allude to his vision of the future. A promise of a new day and a new, liberated ethos is present, for instance, in the endings of *Within the Gates* (1933), *The Star Turns Red* (1940), and, to a lesser degree, *Purple Dust* (1940). Verisimilitude is almost totally abandoned in O'Casey's final Aristophanic allegories; he sketches in the landscape with broad, deft brush work as the Irish playwright reminds us more and more of his vision, of what, ideally, should be. As Robert Hogan has emphasized, these late plays accent the contrast between the paltry, pietistic present and a vanished Golden Age of pastoral joy, freedom, and creative conduct.[17]

Perhaps it is more than coincidental that the same pattern of vacillation—the movement back and forth between the natural and the supernatural—is discernible in many of the poems and plays of William Butler Yeats, the tireless experimenter in verse who refused to accept O'Casey's experimentation in *The Silver Tassie* (1928). Richard Ellmann, for instance, identifies two of the major urges in Yeats' poetry as being a desire to immerse oneself in, or elevate oneself above, the flux of experience.[18] And Yeats himself confesses that much of his early verse was deficient in that it was excessively oriented toward a flight from the real to the ideal, to fairyland:

> I have noticed something about my poetry I did not know before, in this process of correction; for instance, that it is almost all a flight into fairyland from the real world, and a summons to that flight. . . . it is not the poetry of insight and knowledge, but of longing and complaint—the cry of the heart against necessity.[19]

But it is O'Casey's manipulation of these two variables—verisimilitude and vision—which will be our major concern in this book, which concentrates on representative plays from each of O'Casey's three periods: *The Plough and the Stars* (1926) from the Dublin trilogy; *The Silver Tassie*, *Within the Gates*, and *Purple Dust* from the middle plays of extensive experimentation; and *Cock-a-Doodle Dandy* (1949) and *The Drums of Father Ned* (1960), from the last phase.

TWO

IRELAND IN A STATE OF "CHASSIS": THE DUBLIN TRILOGY

A thing that stands demonstrable is that nationhood is not achieved otherwise than in arms: in one or two instances there may have been no actual bloodshed, but the arms were there and the ability to use them. Ireland unarmed will attain just as much freedom as it is convenient for England to give her; Ireland armed will attain ultimately just as much freedom as she wants. . . . We must accustom ourselves to the thought of arms, to the sight of arms, to the use of arms. We may make mistakes in the beginning and shoot the wrong people; but bloodshed is a cleansing and a sanctifying thing, and the nation which regards it as the final horror has lost its manhood. There are many things more horrible than bloodshed; and slavery is one of them. —Padraic Pearse, "The Coming Revolution"

Hundreds of Irishmen did become accustomed to the use of arms in the first quarter of the twentieth century, a belligerent and bloody interlude that saw Irishmen recklessly mounting offensives on several fronts for greater economic and political freedom and cultural identity. The bitterly fought Dublin strike and lockout of 1913, when dynamic Jim Larkin led the exploited Dublin proletariat in a six-month struggle for better wages and working conditions, initiated this period of agitation and unrest; and it was followed by the Easter Week rebellion of 1916, when the Gaelic scholar Padraic Pearse, James Connolly, Sean Mac Diarmada, and others attempted to transform Ireland into a republic free of English control.[1] Civil disorder continued almost without pause until the agreement of January

12, 1922, whereby the Irish Free State came into being as a British dominion, with six counties of northeastern Ireland remaining under British control.

The fear of abrupt displacement, imprisonment, or death was real and recurrent for many Irishmen during this turbulent period in which sabotage, ambushes, lootings, savage reprisal raids, and swift executions became almost daily occurrences in Ireland's nightmarish *agon* for independence and identification.

O'Casey himself vividly evokes the tension and trauma that engulfed his homeland during this time in a paragraph from a letter:

> During this time Ireland was, to quote the Captain in 'Juno,' in a terrible state of 'chassis!' The Celtic twilight exploded into smoky tumult. Armed men in khaki or black, with blackened faces, crouched low in rushing lorries and every whining wail of every passing motor sang of death to someone. Flames from a single rifle lighted a dark street and rifle butts smashed locked doors. Dublin was at war with the British Empire, its regular army and its ruthless ruffians, The Black and Tans. A terrible beauty was in the process of being born.[2]

It is this period of "chassis" (specifically from 1916 to 1923) that provides the historical and atmospheric ethos for O'Casey's three Dublin dramas of lyrical realism, tragicomedies designed to juggle and juxtapose the volatile Irishman's intoxication with his private and political dreams of heroic selfhood (his vivid visions) and his callous disregard of, and antipathy for, his grimy material world (his verisimilitude).

The intermittent struggle in1920 between Republican gunmen and the reckless Black and Tans influences the action in *The Shadow of a Gunman* (1925), a two-act tragedy indicting the Byronic attitudinizing of a dream-addicted poet who proves to be cowardly in the crisis. The guerrilla warfare in the 1920s between the dedicated Republicans, who wanted Ireland free from all British control, and the Civic Guards or Free Staters reflects itself in the events of *Juno and the Paycock* (1925), a tightly-integrated three-act tragedy that records the progressive disintegration of a Dublin tenement family of four, a family destroyed by inescapable economic and political forces and by an admixture of their own vanity, improvidence, and infidelity. And the Easter uprising by the Irish Volunteers and the Irish Citizen Army is the historical reality to which O'Casey is responding in the expansive *The Plough and the Stars* (1926), a Brechtian pageant of doomed revolution as viewed from the windows, steps, and streets of the Dublin slum world.

O'Casey obviously envisions this disorderly sequence of revolutionary episodes as a vast and terrible mass drama. Realizing that he could not possibly resort to documentary realism to chronicle the shifting panorama—the kaleidoscopic array of raids, executions, acrimonious tenement disputes, and street skirmishes—O'Casey judiciously selects certain special moments, pregnant with coarse levity, compassion, and terror, and places them against a background of Dublin proletarian existence. He weaves numerous private crises into his plots, but often these dilemmas are really less significant and terrible than the larger social condition which they interrupt, punctuate, and reflect.[3] Frequently the climaxes in the lives of O'Casey's characters terminate a rising development of tensions, and illuminate the personal tragedies of ordinary people caught within the enclosing net or tangle of historical circumstances. In this sense the private sufferings of individuals emerge as symptomatic recurrences within the revolutionary condition, a conflict that many, particularly the women, had no role in creating. O'Casey's basic dramatic intention in this trilogy emerges, therefore, as an attempt to throw into high and sharp relief the encompassing anarchy, a pervasive disorder that threatens ruin, not to one man (*The Shadow of a Gunman*), or to one family (*Juno and the Paycock*), but to an entire city (*The Plough and the Stars*.)

Agreeing that the broader social tragedy tends to dwarf or minimize individual problems in O'Casey's Dublin trilogy (and in modern tragedy in general), Ronald Peacock observes:

> the individual is overshadowed by the conflict of impersonal forces, of which he is more and more the victim and less and less even so much as the event. . . . A private crisis has little significance for a public eye dazzled by revolution and international vicissitudes. The 'tragic hero' has in consequence disappeared. The tragic plays of O'Casey are symptomatic of this situation. His characters, vivid as some of them are, are not as important as the larger political tragedy of which they are fortuitous victims. In themselves they are not in the least inevitable and unique tragic persons, like those of tradition; any set of Dublin people would do.[4]

Ronald Ayling agrees with Peacock in his evaluation of these Dublin war plays:

> The plays are conceived as social or national tragedies in the widest possible sense, realizing the fearful situation of a whole class, an entire society as much as of individuals like Minnie Powell, Juno Boyle, or Nora Clitheroe. . . . However enjoyable or hilarious the alcoholic fantasies and mock-heroic gestures may be, the moral irresponsibility of the menfolk in each of these early plays is equal in tragic depth to the formal expression of a nation's grief represented in the sufferings of the womenfolk.[5]

Character Defined Against Chaos

The playwright's apparent objective, therefore, in using the fluid Irish war period as recognizable verisimilitude is to focus attention on a general action in which all share by analogy, and that we see adumbrated and interpreted by the individual characters and their relationships, as opposed to the careful and probing scrutiny of one person's quest for safety and survival. O'Casey frequently isolates a character when he is least immersed in his private rationalizations and most open to disinterested insights. The chaos of war unexpectedly invades and interrupts a character's internal debate or his conversation with friends, pulling him into the dangerous vortex of violence and compelling him to manifest certain traits that otherwise might have gone undetected. We are given, therefore, not an Ibsenian or Pirandellian drama of relentless analysis and interrogation, but a robust and raucous drama treating with ensembles, with small, diversified groups of people menaced by social fragmentation. The verisimilitude is truly vertiginous.

Numerous scenes in the plays demonstrate this technique. In *The Shadow of a Gunman*, for example, the Black and Tan raid brings to light the peddler Seumas Shield's superficial piety and false courage; his deferential actions before the Tans show that he does not subscribe to his self-proclaimed belief that religion "makes a man strong in time of trouble."[6] In *Juno and the Paycock*, the thundering rap on the Boyle tenement door by the man in the trench coat in Act I shatters Johnny Boyle's precarious composure and enables us to see that he is, in truth, psychologically handcuffed by fear. In *The Plough and the Stars* the bitter street fighting in Act III brings to the surface the suppressed fear that Jack Clitheroe has tried to mask but must now recognize in the face of his wife's tearful entreaties that he remain with her in the tenement. Also, the killing of Bessie Burgess in the final act of the same play compels Mrs. Gogan to extend tender care to Nora Clitheroe, whom she roundly denounced in Act I as a status-conscious woman with "notions of upperosity." The war provides O'Casey with the means, therefore, to diagnose and chart the anatomy of the Irish character, to expose the Irishman as a strange compact of contending elements with a capacity for cruelty and compassion.[7]

O'Casey is also adept in these early plays in selecting certain scenes, those quiet moments in his characters' lives, which often follow interludes of heroic bombast or violence, when they perceive their perilous immediate situation and fret about the uncertain future. Donal Davoren experiences such a moment of awareness in the curtain scene in *The Shadow of a Gunman*, lamenting, "It's terrible to think that little Minnie is dead, but it's still more terrible to think that Davoren and Shields are alive!"[8] Fluther Good, O'Casey's bibulous and loquacious carpenter, has a similar moment of awareness in the last act of *The Plough and the Stars* when, conscious of the dead bodies inside and the glare of the burning buildings outside, he declares to the Covey that he is going to drink all of his whiskey now because "How th' hell does a fella know there'll be any tomorrow?"[9] In the same act, similar thoughtful moments are shared by Captain Brennan, Peter Flynn, Sergeant Tinley, and Nora Clitheroe. In this manner O'Casey contrives to capture the larger general action behind the trilogy—the frantic efforts to survive in the midst of civil strife—from numerous vantage points, using a diversified cast of Irishmen as human reflectors, without enunciating an explicit thesis.

Because O'Casey is attempting to embody dramatically the enveloping action from many different points of view, his Dublin plays tend to resemble prisms. The separate acts are roughly analogous to the sides of a prism, reflecting and dispersing sharp, bright colors emanating from the center of flaming disorder in the city. Each play resembles, then, a human spectrum, with each character serving as a special filter and giving his own personal coloration to the central situation that is revealed through him. It is, then, a verisimilitude both vivid and variegated.

O'Casey's comic, exuberantly romantic lower class characters are virtually all involved in different ways in the general situation, the agitation. The strife promises to preserve or destroy certain personal, political, economic, religious, and social values precious to every member of the dramatis personae. The war presents Jack Clitheroe and other Irish soldiers, caught up in the jingoistic frenzy of the moment, with chances for personal fame and military advancement. Conversely, the war threatens to shatter the homes of Nora Clitheroe and Juno Boyle, whom O'Casey describes as "a true hero, though unhonored and unsung."[10] The strife provides Bessie Burgess and her rabble army, which descends with prams upon the unprotected shops and stores, with opportunities for pillage; and the unrest supplies Peter Flynn, Tommy Owens, and other false patriots with numerous chances for patriotic boasting and heroic masquerade.

As the people stand in sharp relief against the landscape of red ruin, O'Casey concerns himself, therefore, with achieving a two-fold objective. First, he wants to trace in the foreground their personal, often exasperating, confrontations and collisions as they meet only to fly apart. Second, he wants to record their constantly shifting reactions to, and appraisals of, the ebb and flow of battle in the background. The characters are indeed agitated by divided allegiances—by their direct, immediate involvement in personal struggles, and by their indirect and intermittent preoccupation with the sometimes distant, sometimes close, impersonal force. With this complex mode of dramaturgy, O'Casey is able to give us life in depth, intimate and intense, and in breadth, as the apprehensive members of the Irish microcosm react differently to the pressures of civil tumult.

THE PLOUGH AND THE STARS: VAIN IRISHMEN WITH VISIONS

O'Casey's *The Plough and the Stars*, the most sophisticated work in the trilogy and a masterfully modulated dramatic orchestration fusing the argumentative arias of a mad motley—an Irish microcosm—with the booming, cacophonous uproar of a city under siege, certainly introduces us to an ensemble that is both fascinated with and frightened by the risks and red fires of revolution. Assembling a cross-section of tenement

Dubliners who drank, whored, boasted, gambled, looted, fought, and died in the Easter Week uprising, O'Casey, with an admirable combination of sympathy and detachment, traces the mushrooming movement of nationalistic frenzy—the Irish bottle and battle cry—that ignites an explosive revolution, a hopeless war, which slowly encircles and then penetrates to disperse or destroy the remaining tenement dwellers.

With his microcosmic approach to the situation, O'Casey gives us ten evocative specimens, ten compressed but illuminating vignettes of a bricklayer, his young, socially ambitious wife, a laborer, a fitter, a street fruit-vendor, a charwoman, her consumptive child, a carpenter, a chicken butcher, and a prostitute, plus quick, revealing glimpses of various members of the Irish and English military establishments. Extracting numerous individual disputes and disasters from the lives of these people, who scurry back and forth against an exploding conflagration—colliding with, cursing, and consoling each other in crazy configurations of conduct—O'Casey integrates these private dilemmas into a mosaic more superbly varied and vivid than that of either of the two previous plays. The dramatist adroitly exploits the central, exasperating predicament—the danger and discomfort of many personages in the face of possible ruin—to reveal certain basic human traits and to remind us continually of the disorder that is impinging. Indeed, the slum world in this play resembles, at moments, a relatively small island in a sea of violence, which first beats against, and finally inundates, the ugly, disfigured tenement city.

O'Casey certainly concentrates upon verisimilitude in this play, describing in detail the exterior and interior—the domestic clutter and confinement—of the long, gaunt five-story tenement that houses the Clitheroes and their curious relatives and neighbors. Nora Clitheroe, for example, describes the tenement apartments as "vaults . . . that are hidin' th' dead, instead of homes that are sheltherin' th' livin'."[11] Thus the clinical exactness and completeness of his stage settings remind one of similar descriptions in the plays of Gerhart Hauptmann, especially *The Weavers* (1892). O'Casey's objective in reproducing the minutiae of Dublin ghetto life is, with some major reservations, identical with that of Émile Zola and the French naturalists: O'Casey is intent upon presenting a sociological study of background with a multitude of individuals being modified, both physically and psychologically, by their oppressive milieu. Like Zola, O'Casey is also ultimately concerned with social reform—with the removal of the evils that prevent man from enjoying a healthy and productive life.

Yet the vision is present to militate against the verisimilitude, and it is the Figure in the Window, a slow-striding silhouette of extended, elevated utterance, who dreams (in the Act II tavern scene) of an attainable future far superior to the disorderly, disorganized present. A dedicated revolutionary willing to die for his country, the Figure, using passages from Padraic Pearse's speeches, asserts that arms in the hands of Irishmen is a glorious sight, and that the shedding of blood is a cleansing, sanctifying act. Insisting that Irishmen gladly give their lives for the love of their country, pouring out their red blood in sacrifice, he urges them to welcome war as if it were an Angel of God. With his revolutionary zeal and total commitment to his cause, the Figure, with his plea for unity of action, is clearly inspired by a vision of a "redeemed" and liberated Ireland.

This vision of a redeemed Ireland has extraordinary appeal for the clamoring, drinking Irish insurgents because it diverts their attention from the lice and litter that they would like to ignore in their tenement homes, the depressing real. Moreover, the Figure's appeal excites the histrionic rebels because it hints at the possibility of glory, of heroic achievement, to be gained in battle; it is a temptation that few of the warriors can resist because they are basically egocentric, vain men, more concerned with private advancement than with public progress.

Refusing to consider seriously the prospect of confronting

a larger, disciplined English force in open battle, the insurgents, instead, behave like a gang of petulant, jealous schoolboys in a game of make-believe war; they worry about a rival's recent promotion or about the kind of figure they cut in their uniforms. As W. A. Armstrong points out: "The vanity of the patriots is especially apparent in their excessive love of picturesque regalia and military rank."[12] This vanity animates old and young alike. Peter Flynn spends most of his time preparing to attend torchlight parades around monuments of Irish patriots, or making patriotic pilgrimages to Wolfe Tone's grave. It is his outlandish Forester uniform—frilled shirt, white breeches, top boots, a green coat with gold braid, a slouch hat with ostrich plume, and a sword—that prompts the Covey to describe him as "th' illegitimate son of an illegitimate child of a corporal in th' Mexican Army!"[13] Jack Clitheroe is equally guilty of playing to the grandstand In Act I Fluther observes that Jack is very fond of his gun and his Citizen Army badge of the Red Hand. Mrs. Gogan adds later that Clitheroe was so certain that he would be promoted to captain that "he bought a Sam Browne belt, an' was always puttin' it on an' standin' at the door showing it off, till th' man came an' put out the street lamps on him. God, I think he used to bring it to bed with him!"[14]

Ultimately it is the exasperated Nora, who had destroyed the letter notifying Jack that he had been promoted to commandant in the Citizen Army, who screams at Jack—in a speech of prophecy at the close of Act I—that his vanity will eventually destroy both him and his family:

> NORA (flaming up). I burned it, I burned it! That's what I did with it! Is General Connolly an' th' Citizen Army goin' to be your only care? Is your home goin' to be only a place to rest in? Am I goin' to be only somethin' to provide merry-makin' at night for you? Your vanity'll be th' ruin of you an' me yet . . . That's what's movin' you: because they've made an officer of you, you'll make a glorious cause of what you're doin', while

> your little red-lipp'd Nora can go on sittin' here, makin' a companion of th' loneliness of th' night![15]

Perhaps it is more than sheer coincidence that O'Casey's young slum wife, with her vision of a happy home amidst slum sordidness, resembles another frustrated young wife with the same first name—the Nora Helmer of Henrik Ibsen's *A Doll's House* (1879). Like Ibsen's maturing wife and mother, O'Casey's Nora resents being treated like a pretty plaything, like a live doll who merely exists to satisfy the passionate whims of her demanding husband and to nurture the myth of masculine superiority. Desiring joyful reciprocity and mutual respect in marriage, both Noras exert themselves to protect their husbands: Ibsen's Nora commits forgery to save her husband's career, and O'Casey's Nora endangers her life in a foolish attempt to coax her husband home from the barricades used in the street fighting. The ideal of democratic family comradeship eludes both Noras, however, because the wife walks out in Ibsen's play and the husband—to his death—in O'Casey's.

If O'Casey suspected some of the insurgents' reasons for participation in Ireland's confused struggle for freedom, he was dismayed by their battle tactics. In his autobiography, O'Casey reveals that many Irish Citizen Army men "were immersed in the sweet illusion of fluttering banners, of natty uniforms, bugle-blown marches, with row on row of dead and dying foemen strewn over the Macgillicuddy's Reeks, the Hills of Dublin, and the bonny blue Mountains of Mourne, with the *Soldier's Song* aroaring at the dawning of the day. All guns and drums, but no wounds."[16] As secretary of the Council of the Irish Citizen Army, O'Casey had championed guerrilla warfare—swift hit-and-run tactics by Irishmen in drab, ordinary clothing, a modified application of the Boer method of fighting. Ironically, it is the uniform-loving Captain Brennan who must don civilian clothes to effect his escape in the last act of the play.

Identifying *The Plough and the Stars* as a tragedy of vanity, O'Casey comments on the contrast between the "Orator" and his listeners in this paragraph from a letter:

> I think so, though there is many-sided vanities in the work; of the Covey, of Pete Flynn, of the brave Bessie, of the equally brave Fluther; of Clitheroe and his companion captain. We have all some vanity or other; but mostly innocent ones; remaining innocent so long as we refuse to allow it to destroy or weaken our finer qualities. But the 'Orator' is not vain; he is dangerous[ly] sincere; so sure that he is ready to kill or be killed for his Ideal, as many great men were—Washington, Lincoln, Kosciusko. I knew this 'orator' well—Padraic Pearse, and there were none more charming, gentle or brave than he.[17]

O'CASEY'S POLYPHONIC PROCEDURE

If O'Casey's thematic focus is virtually identical with that of the two previous plays—disgust with slum life, reckless armed conflict, and Irish irrationality—his technique is not. Indeed, there is significant advance in the *modus operandi*—the technical strategy—of this third play, in which O'Casey resorts to an "interwoven" or "polyphonic" method. For instance, he constantly shifts from one dilemma and one set of characters to another, sometimes delaying (indeed, neglecting) completion of a sequence of events that has captured our attention. The adventure that we are following is likely at any moment to be interrupted by some unanticipated incident, and so we gradually get the impression that silly or savage episodes are going on simultaneously all around us.

At the close of Act I, for example, O'Casey gives Mollser, the frail child of the slums, a brief scene with Nora, and our interest in this uneven battle between the shriveled child of about fifteen (who is terribly afraid that she will die some time when she is by herself) and the slum world is immediately engaged; we are worried, but hope that she survives. However, we do not see Mollser at all in Act II, and only briefly in Act III. We must wait until the very last act to learn that she has died. In Act III O'Casey abruptly introduces a fashionably dressed, middle-aged woman who, almost fainting with fear, asks Peter Flynn's aid in fleeing the strife-torn slum area. Before we can discover what happens to the lady, who wanders off in a despairing, aimless fashion, Mrs. Gogan, Bessie, and Peter spill out of the tenement to disappear from view as they race to join the others in the looting of shops. Later in the same act O'Casey rivets our attention on Lieutenant Langon who, with his stomach punctured with wounds, is hauled into the tenement by his comrades who are fleeing the bloody melee in the street. Our fear increases as we watch the lieutenant writhe in pain and utter his cries of anguish. Then, suddenly, before Langon's ordeal is completed, O'Casey directs our attention to a bitter quarrel taking place between Jack and Nora as the latter tries desperately to cling to her terrified husband in an effort to prevent him from returning to the fighting. A new action has been initiated before the old one is finished, and we never know whether the lieutenant survived his wounds. This interruption of one private drama by another, frequently at a tense, critical moment, is recurrent in this third play, as the farcical and the pathetic succeed one another in a rapid, swirling fashion.

This dramatic method, while reminding us of melodramas and the movies, anticipates the technical strategies of anecdotal arrangement and reflexive reference used so extensively by Ezra Pound in the "Cantos" and James Joyce in *Ulysses*.[18] Basically, the anecdotal method is discernible when an anecdote or embryonic situation is initiated in one section and then abruptly dropped; it is reactivated in one or more subsequent passages, being finally disposed of in a later segment. It is the tactic of deliberate disconnectedness; the writer engages our attention and then disconcerts us by introducing new and disjunct material or by reverting to the old. When this disconnectedness occurs, the sequential advance is momentarily stalled as the writer cuts back and forth among the various threads of action, frequently working in a steadily rising, powerful crescendo, such as the one that occurs at the close of Act II in *The Plough and the Stars*.

When a writer such as O'Casey employs the anecdotal technique he frustrates the reader's normal expectation of an easily followed sequence and compels him to perceive the elements of his play as being juxtaposed in space while they are advancing in time. *The Plough and the Stars* is a series of isolated fragments, each of which exposes some aspect of the central revolutionary dilemma. There is a perceptible framework—the war—around which the seemingly disconnected episodes are organized; the fragmentary events are focused on the uprising, and yet the reader continually is forced to fit the many fragments together until, by reflexive reference, he can perceive them as a meaningful, mosaic pattern.

The Irish dramatist, therefore, utilizes in this work a structure that depends upon the perception of relationships that are ostensibly unrelated. Yet to be comprehended completely, these relationships must be held in suspension and then assembled by the reader or viewer with the drama's completion. The process of recognition and reference for individual, component parts must embrace the entire play, and only then can the entire complex of internal references be apprehended as a unit. Like Joyce, O'Casey sought to achieve the same unified impact, the same sense of simultaneous activity occurring in different locales, and so he moved back and forth among the various areas of action, frequently aiming for an ironic effect, as when he jumps from prostitute to patriot in Act II. Hence *The Plough and the Stars* impresses as a masterpiece of the unification of disparate ideas and emotions, a dramatic entity requiring a retentive and creative responsiveness from the reader or play goer.

Four Acts of Fear and Fury

The drama has four acts. Act I hints at the gathering storm as the Irish heroes don their uniforms; Act II studies the assembled heroes on parade as they carry flags, lift glasses, listen to oratory, and hurl threats at the enemy; Act III shows them facing, or running from, battle; and Act IV gives us the tragic aftermath—the emotional letdown—as the fighting tapers off. Robert Hogan comments upon the expanding-contracting pattern of the play:

> Spatially, the play is an expansion and a retraction. In the Exposition, the characters are confined to the tenement. In the Development, they revolt, emerge from the tenement, and invade the outside world. In the Reversal, they are driven back to the street in front of the tenement. In the Resolution, they have been driven back inside the tenement, and during the act they are driven further, until finally there is no room for them anywhere. Stoddart and Tinley dispossess or kill them and hold the tenement alone.[19]

Act I, set in the home of the Clitheroes ("a fine old Georgian house, struggling for its life against the assaults of time, and the still more savage assaults of the tenants"),[20] is designed to introduce and characterize all of the major and most of the minor characters, isolating their shallow hatreds, serious fears, and dreams; to study the mounting antagonism between Nora and Jack, which forms the major plot complication; to convey the impression of social confusion; and to foreshadow subsequent violent events. O'Casey shows great skill in tracing the movement of impulsive feeling as irritation and sympathy break forth in rapid alternation among the Clitheroes, Peter Flynn, Fluther, the young Covey, Mollser, Bessie Burgess, and Mrs. Gogan.

Peter Flynn, Fluther, and the young Covey engage in much of the verbal fencing. In one instance, the men repairing the street in front of the Clitheroe apartment give a loud cheer, throw down their tools, and depart—actions that prepare for Covey's immediate appearance. Wearing dungarees and a vivid, red tie, he enters to report that work has been halted and the workers mobilized to march under the Plough and the Stars in that night's patriotic demonstration. With his strong faith in Darwinian evolutionary theory and Marxian dialectic, the young Covey at first irritates Fluther with his criticism of religion, and the carpenter vigorously replies:

> FLUTHER. You'll be kickin' an' yellin' for th' priest yet, me boyo. I'm not goin' to stand silent an' simple listenin' to a thick like you makin' a maddenin' mockery o' God Almighty. It 'ud be a nice derogatory thing on me conscience, an' me dyin', to look back in rememberin' shame of talkin' to a word-weavin' little ignorant yahoo of a red flag Socialist![21]

Moments later the young Covey provokes Peter by tossing his discarded dungarees on top of Peter's white shirt; a farcical fight ensues, with Peter brandishing his sword and chasing the young Covey around the table and out of the room. Nora's entrance halts the silly squabble; she lectures the two men about their behavior, asserting to Covey: "Jack'll be in any minute, an' I'm not goin' to have th' quiet of his evenin' tossed about in an everlastin' uproar between you an' Uncle Pether."[22] Later Nora, after helping her uncle don his ceremonial garb, gently pushes him out of the tenement. Armstrong observes: "Nora Clitheroe makes his vanity seem like that of a small boy when she buckles his sword for him, puts his hat on his head, and hurries him out of the house."[23]

A brief love scene between Jack and Nora follows, but the

outside world invades when Captain Brennan enters to give Jack a dispatch from General Connolly informing Jack that he is to command the eighth battalion of the I.C.A. Jack then discovers that he was promoted to commandant two weeks prior to the current orders, but that Nora destroyed the communique. A bitter argument follows and Jack, after grabbing his Sam Browne belt, revolver, and hat, departs with Brennan, an exit that anticipates the closing events of Act II. Moments later, Mollser, temporarily abandoned by her mother, who has gone to the demonstration, enters to assert ironically that she envies Nora because the latter has such a nicely furnished and happy home. Then, as the Dublin Fusiliers march down the tenement streets singing lustily "It's a Long Way to Tipperary," Bessie closes the act by predicting the ruin that must follow: "they'll be scattered abroad, like th' dust in the darkness!"[24]

PROSTITUTE AND PATRIOT

The rampant emotionalism continues in Act II, which is designed to reveal a Dublin crowd's mesmerization by nationalistic oratory, to heighten the play's implicit feeling of danger, and to extend the drama's scope by including a greater number of people and events off stage. O'Casey uses a divided stage in this act. Most of the action takes place in a "commodious public-house" with a tall, wide, two-paned window at the back, through which a rebel leader may be seen and heard as he paces back and forth on a platform, addressing the patriotic demonstrators and assembled troops. The opening scene involves the Barman and a prostitute, Rosie Redmond, who complains that business is off because the men have their minds on higher things than a girl's "garthers." Her description of the group as "th' glorious company of th' saints, an' the noble army of martyrs thrampin' through th' sthreets of paradise"[25] foreshadows the death of Jack and the other insurgents.

Rosie also performs another vital function, as William Butler Yeats indicates in this defense of the scene and Rosie's conduct:

> She is certainly as necessary to the general action and idea as the drunkards and wastrels. O'Casey is contrasting the ideal dream with the normal grossness of life and of that she is an essential part. It is no use putting her in if she does not express herself vividly and in character, if her 'professional' side is not emphasized.[26]

An extended cavalcade of wild comic scenes follows as the passionate, bombastic utterances of the swilling, milling Irish mob, Peter, Fluther, Covey, Bessie, and Mrs. Gogan included, mingle in point-counterpoint with the grandiose, balanced rhetoric of the speaker outside. Fluther adequately summarizes the reckless mood of the crowd:

> FLUTHER. Jammed as I was in th' crowd, I listened to th' speeches pattherin' on th' people's heads, like rain fallin' on th' corn; every derogatory thought went out o' me mind, an' I said to meself, 'You can die now, Fluther, for you've seen th' shadow-dhreams of th' past leppin' to life in th' bodies of livin' men that show, if we're without a titther o' courage for centuries, we're vice versa now!' Looka here. (He stretches out his arm under Peter's face and rolls up his sleeve.) The blood was BOILIN' in me veins![27]

Later Covey declaims about economic freedom and Jenersky's *Thesis on the Origin, Development, and Consolidation of the Evolutionary Idea of the Proletariat;* Peter boasts of his prayer book, packed with leaves from Wolfe Tone's grave; Bessie worries about her son with the Tommies in Europe; Mrs. Gogan slanders Bessie; and the Barman, as the cursing, scuffling, and drinking increase, fears for another endorsement on his license. Meanwhile, the orator outside pleads for *unity* of belief and action from the Irish Volunteers and the Citizen Army men; it is these assorted noncombatants and camp followers who make a mockery of patriotism by their contemptible conduct. So this is realism distinguished by Chaucerian gusto and Hogarthian candor.

Near the end of the act, Clitheroe, Captain Brennan, and Lieutenant Langon of the Irish Volunteers enter the public house, and O'Casey describes the trio: "They are in a state of emotional excitement. Their faces are flushed and their eyes sparkle; they speak rapidly, as if unaware of the meaning of what they said. They have been mesmerized by the fervency of the speeches."[28] Lifting glasses and waving flags, the men exclaim in antiphonal fashion:

LIEUT. LANGON. Th' time is rotten ripe for revolution.
CLITHEROE. You have a mother, Langon.
LIEUT. LANGON. Ireland is greater than a mother.
CAPTAIN BRENNAN. You have a wife, Clitheroe.
CLITHEROE. Ireland is greater than a wife.[29]

Jack's declaration foreshadows his behavior in the crisis when he cruelly deserts his wife in the street to return to die for Kathleen ni Houlihan. Armstrong suggests that this scene reveals "the moral inadequacy of the intoxicated patriotism which makes Clitheroe, Brennan, and Langon renounce filial and marital bonds so grandiloquently."[30] Clitheroe predicts his own end with the cry "Death for th' Independence of Ireland!,"[31] and then rushes out with the others as a bugle blows Assembly. The act ends as the drunken Fluther and Rosie emerge from the snug on their way home for a night of pleasure.

The Blood-Dimmed Tide Is Loosed

The tumultuous Act III takes place in the street outside the Clitheroe home during the Easter Week of 1916. The act starts slowly and on a subdued note as Mrs. Gogan seats her weakened daughter outside to catch the wan rays of the sun, but it quickly gains momentum as the sardonic gallows-humor gives way to a steadily expanding tragic mood. O'Casey's satiric mockery of those civilians who race about spreading rumors, stealing goods, and interfering with the Irish rebels' attempts to defeat the English—behaving like excited schoolboys watching a thrilling game that doesn't directly concern them—only serves to augment the ironic intensity of the later cluster of tragic events. Mrs. Gogan's remarks to the young Covey and Peter, who enter breathless and excited early in the act, are fairly typical of the exaggerated reports circulating through the tenement world:

> MRS. GOGAN. (to the two men). Were yous far up th' town? Did yous see any sign o' Fluther or Nora? How is things lookin'? I hear they're blazin' away out o' th' G.P.O. That th' Tommies is sthretched in heaps around Nelson's Pillar an' th' Parnell Statue, an' that th' pavin' sets in O'Connell Street is nearly covered be pools o' blood.[32]

As the fighting mounts in intensity, with the gunboat *Helga* lobbing large shells on the embattled Irish, a second army—equipped with prams, boxes, and sacks—descends upon the unprotected shops. The slum dwellers' stockpiling of hats, umbrellas, biscuits, flour, ham, boots, tables, chairs, and whiskey is subsequently interrupted by the arrival in the tenement of Captain Brennan, the wounded Lieutenant Langon, and the pale, frightened Clitheroe, all three fleeing the converging British forces. Jack, momentarily forgetting his vanity and speaking honestly, tells his wife that he wishes he had never left her. Looking on from above, Bessie, as one-woman chorus, volunteers her usual caustic appraisal of the situation:

> BESSIE (from the upper window). Th' Minsthrel Boys aren't feelin' very comfortable now. Th' big guns has knocked all th' harps out of their hands. General Clitheroe'd rather be unlacin' his wife's bodice than standin' at the barricade. . . . An th'

> professor of chicken-butcherin' there, finds he's up against somethin' a little tougher even than his own chickens, an' that's saying a lot![33]

Bessie's depreciatory speech alludes to a well-known Irish ballad about a heroic Irish lad, "The Minstrel Boy":

> The minstrel boy to the war is gone,
>   In the ranks of death you will find him,
> His father's sword he has girded on,
>   And his wild harp slung behind him.
> "Land of song!" said the warrior bard,
>   "Though all the world betrays thee,
> *One* sword, at least, thy rights shall guard,
>   *One* faithful harp shall praise thee!"
>
> The minstrel fell!—but the foeman's chain
>   Could not bring his proud soul under;
> The harp he loved n'er spoke again,
>   For he tore its chords asunder;
> And said, "No chains shall sully thee,
>   Thou soul of love and bravery!
> Thy songs were made for the pure and free,
>   They shall never sound in slavery!"[34]

The implications, mostly ironic, stemming from Bessie's reference to this sentimental Irish ballad-poem are numerous. First, the song presents sympathetically the figure of the courageous, joyful Irish lad who, though lacking the physical and mental maturity of an older man, seizes his father's sword and departs to oppose the foeman who would despoil his native land, the citadel of freedom. The minstrel boy perishes in battle, dismantling his harp, the symbol of joyful song and valiant conduct (indeed, of Ireland herself), so that his oppressive captors could not use it when they chanted their victorious songs in the newly subjugated land. The ballad conveys, therefore, an image of a time past, of a heroic age when Irish men, even minstrel boys, willingly sacrificed their lives in battle in an unsuccessful but admirable struggle to defend their homeland and escape slavery.

The ballad has reverse connotations when applied to the immediate, fluid situation and the bewildered rebels in the play. Unlike the minstrel boy, O'Casey's slum warriors are running in despair—not advancing with patriotic fervor and determination—from battle. They have discovered that it takes real courage and stamina to wield men's weapons (the fathers' swords) in the battle to escape bondage. In their confusion and fear, they remind us of the fraudulent, mock patriot Peter Flynn, who earlier girded on an oversize sword that he never intended to use. O'Casey seems bent on conveying the impression that Jack and the others are boy-men, unable to handle the weapons of war and thereby defend their country's honor, symbolized in the harp. Unlike the heroic minstrel boy, O'Casey's fighters have lost their proud souls—the strong pride in themselves and their country that was so apparent in earlier acts—in the face of the foeman's ball and chain.

Consequently, they do not redeem the harp (Ireland) or themselves through valiant actions; they run for cover or die in foolish and cowardly desperation. It is the victorious foemen, the British, who remain to sing the songs of love and bravery, as the two British tea-drinkers do in the play's curtain scene. Thus O'Casey's false minstrel boys, the warrior bards of the Dublin pubs, also join the ranks of the defeated, and the songs for the pure and brave are sung by the foemen who have claimed, indeed sullied, the Irish harp. Hence O'Casey uses this traditional ballad to foreshadow later events and to underscore his denigrating portrait of the Irish rebels.

Despite his wife's entreaties for him to remain, Jack departs with Brennan to rejoin the fighting, the catastasis of the drama. Jack's brutal rejection of his wife, who collapses weakly on the street, moves Bessie to carry Nora into the house (Nora is beginning to experience early birth pains). As Fluther, who has entered with a woman's vivid blue hat on his head and an earthen half-gallon jar of whiskey in his arms, sings in his drunken frenzy, and Nora screams in pain, Bessie, leaving Mrs. Gogan to attend Nora, moves off through the sound of rifle shots, and the "tok, tok, tok" of a distant machine gun in quest of a doctor, as the act ends.

No More Dancing to a Frenzied Drum

Act IV, which records the exhausted, subdued, tenement dwellers' persistent and pathetic efforts to survive the mopping-up operations initiated by the British, is set in the cramped attic living room of Bessie Burgess, who is attending the irrational Nora. It is dusk and the room is dark except for the limited light provided by the fire, and by two candles situated on a stool near a coffin that rests on two kitchen chairs. Through one small rear window, the glare of the burning buildings in the town is visible. Robert Hogan observes:

> The tone is subdued. The characters have grown torpid; even the running war between the Covey and Peter is muted. All of them are concerned with the effects of the war and with the working out of their own personal destinies. The comic appeared in earlier acts when characters seemed to control their destinies; in this act, their destinies are controlled externally, and their individuality and high spirits are muted. [35]

Extreme quiet prevails in the very early moments as Peter, Fluther, and the young Covey sit on the floor playing cards. As they argue over the game and listen to Nora's feeble moans from the bedroom and the cries for a Red Cross ambulance in the street, they disclose that Nora's baby, which was born dead, has been placed in the coffin with Mollser, who has finally succumbed to consumption. They also comment on the great risk involved in standing near windows that are constantly being shattered by the English soldiers, alert for Irish snipers.

Then Captain Brennan, dressed in civilian clothing and groggy with fatigue, arrives to report that Jack has perished in the fighting at the Imperial Hotel, a major spire of tension in the denouement:

> CAPT. BRENNAN. He took it like a man. His last whisper was to 'tell Nora to be brave; that I'm ready to meet God, an' that I'm proud to die for Ireland.' An' when our General heard it he said that 'Commandant Clitheroe's end was a gleam of glory.' Mrs. Clitheroe's grief will be a joy when she realizes that she has had a hero for a husband.[36]

Nora is unable, however, to realize anything. When she enters, with the light of incipient insanity showing in her eyes, she imagines that she is in the country with Jack. Later, in action reminiscent of Ophelia's "mad" scene in *Hamlet*, she arranges the table for tea while she sings a romantic song about violets, a robin, and love.

O'Casey apparently had Shakespeare's young woman in mind in shaping this scene—indeed, in arranging Nora's tragic predicament—because the careers of Ophelia and Nora are somewhat similar. Perhaps the most obvious feature is that both young women are shattered by lost love. Ophelia's decline begins when she loses Hamlet's affection; later, the loss of her father, Polonius, removes the second major emotional prop, and she finds herself alienated from those she holds most dear. Since she has relied heavily upon sweetheart and father for support and protection, she is ill-equipped to survive in isolation. Hence, when her sheltered world is disrupted, she collapses into irrationality. Lacking strength of character, she cannot cope with grim reality, although her bawdy songs, lilted in her madness, indicate that she has some insight into the harsh, sometimes sordid real world.

The Nora of Dublin, the second testament in madness, is like Ophelia in that she works to create and then to defend an idyllic world of love and order; she will extend—make permanent—the honeymoon bliss. She, too, begins to lose her optimism and composure when her husband rejects her for the military; she hastens her collapse with unwise actions, finding, like Ophelia, temporary joy in the phantasmagoria of impermanence. Unlike the gentle, passive Ophelia, Nora does not, however, surrender to death; as a product of the Dulin slums, she is relatively self-reliant, and we are left with some slight hope that she may yet regain her mental equilibrium. In the face of successive and severe emotional jolts, both women, therefore, experience a rising hysteria and despair, recoiling in shocked disbelief as their dream worlds are first invaded and then fragmented. As a consequence, they react as temperament and training dictate: the stronger woman of the slums survives the mood of fatigue and frenetic emotionalism, but the gentle, aristocratic lady of the court is crushed.

The chanting appeal for the Red Cross, a burst of rifle fire, and the rapid fire of a machine gun shatter Nora's pleasant delirium, and she screams for her husband and baby from a window she has frantically opened. When Bessie, who has been sleeping heavily by the fire, rushes to pull Nora from the window, she (Bessie) is shot:

> BESSIE. (with an arrested scream of fear and pain). Merciful God, I'm shot, I'm shot, I'm shot! . . . Th' life's pourin' out o' me! (To Nora) I've got this through . . . through you . . . through you, you bitch, you! . . . O God, have mercy on me! . . . (To Nora) You wouldn't stop quiet, no, you wouldn't, you wouldn't, blast you! Look at what I'm afther gettin', look at what I'm afther gettin' . . . I'm bleedin' to death, an' no one's here to stop th' flowin' blood! (Calling) Mrs. Gogan, Mrs. Gogan! Fluther, Fluther, for God's sake, somebody, a doctor, a doctor![37]

Mrs. Gogan hastily reenters—followed seconds later by Stoddart and Tinley, their rifles at the ready—to lead the shattered Nora out, the latter whimperingly declaring that she can't bear to look at Bessie's lifeless body. The curtain falls as the two soldiers, sipping the tea that the demented wife had desired for her dead husband and ignoring the sheet-covered body of Bessie, join in the chorus of "Keep The Home Fires Burning" that their comrades are singing at a barricade in the street:

Sergeant Tinley and Corporal Stoddart (joining in the chorus as they sip the tea):

> Keep the 'owme fires burning,
> While your 'earts are yearning;
> Though your lads are far away
> They dream of 'owme;
> There's a silver loining
> Through the dark cloud shoining,
> Turn the dark cloud inside out,
> Till the boys come 'owme![38]

The curtain scene compounds the ironies, and commingles verisimilitude and vision in a powerful manner, as the sentimental soldiers' song radiates two distinctly different implications when applied to the victors and to the vanquished. First, the soldiers sing, not because they are happy, but because, weary of war, they are sad and homesick. They are the lads who are far away and who look for the silver lining, which is symbolic of the advent of a new era of peace. They sing to the mothers and wives who are attending the hearth fires in England. They sing because they have reason to hope that they will eventually be going home. The reverse is true when the Irish, especially Nora, are considered. Like many other Irish wives and mothers, Nora struggled rationally and recklessly to keep the fire burning in her home. Now the cheerful warmth of a home fire is being enjoyed by two of the enemy soldiers who destroyed her husband in a much larger fire. Jack is but one of the many Irish boys who won't be coming home. Finally, there is irony and unintentional brutality in the two soldiers' plea to "keep the 'owme fires burning" when we view it against a city in which many Irish homes are being gutted and leveled by fire.

O'CASEY'S EARLY MASTERPIECE

As a kaleidoscopic pageant of reckless revolution in a filth-stained and fragmenting slum world, *The Plough and the Stars* shows how impassioned and militant nationalism disrupts family and community life. Armstrong suggests that one of the basic, recurrent themes is "the way in which the vanity and excitements created by patriotism and war disrupt and destroy fundamental human relationships, particularly those between husband and wife, and those between mother and child."[39] He points out that in Act I Jack deserts his wife, and Mrs. Gogan her daughter, to attend military and patriotic meetings; in Act II Mrs. Gogan's interest in the great rally causes her temporarily to abandon her baby on the floor of the public house; and in Act III Mrs. Gogan again leaves her baby and her tubercular daughter, in order to loot shops, while Jack again harshly rejects his hysterical wife.

It is perhaps worthwhile to point out that O'Casey's third play effectively supports, indeed emphasizes, many of Henri Bergson's views on vanity:

> Probably there is not a single failing that is more superficial or more deep-rooted. The wounds it receives are never serious, and yet they are seldom healed. The services rendered to it are the most unreal of services, and yet they are the very ones that meet with lasting gratitude. . . . It is scarcely a vice, and yet all the vices are drawn into its orbit and, in proportion as they become more refined and artificial, tend to be nothing more than a means of satisfying it. . . . True modesty can be nothing but a meditation on vanity. . . . It is a sort of scientific cautiousness to respect what we shall say and think of ourselves. It is made of improvements and aftertouches. In short, it is an acquired virtue.[40]

The vanity of the rebels was, indeed, deep-rooted, prompting them to suffer and die in the performance of unrealistic services. Losing their perspective, they attempted to utilize uniforms, guns, songs, lights, mirrors, public gatherings, drink, even people, to gratify their vain desires, their visions. Like a powerful magnet attracting particles of iron, the romantic monomania of men like Clitheroe quickly assembled adjunctory vices: arrogance, valiant fury, irascibility, and indifference, to cite but a few. Modesty was, so Bergson suggests, a virtue they needed to acquire, although the Irish nation, quickly forgetting their defects, rewarded them with immediate and intense expressions of gratitude, quickly elevating them to the roles of heroes and martyrs.

In holding the mirror up to revolution, *The Plough and the Stars* holds in suspension all of the dramaturgical devices of O'Casey's maturing artistry. The plot design is not linear, as in the previous two plays, but centripetal. The characters collide, move apart, only to meet again; O'Casey manifests artful artlessness in presenting the flow and commingling of lives. Often the characters, absorbed in their own private dilemmas or worried about the violence about them, rub against each other with that destructive casualness and callousness so common in tense situations. In Act II, for example, Peter Flynn and Covey barely pause to jibe at each other as they rush in and out of the tavern; in the same act, Fluther, Peter, and the young Covey forget the ailing Nora and ignore the shelling of the G.P.O. to toss coins; in Act IV Captain Brennan deserts his doomed comrades to play cards in Bessie's flat; and in the same act Corporal Stoddart, amidst the cursing and clutter, nonchalantly declares that the "dawg-foight," as he calls it, is about over.

The use of sound effects and stage illumination is more extensive and effective than in the two previous works. Commenting upon the incipient expressionism in the play—the large groupings of characters, the sounds of marching feet, a brass band, soldiers singing, and the interweaving of the "lilting" chant with ballads and hymns, Vincent C. DeBaun concludes: "Bessie's witch-like appearance in Act I after the chorus of 'Tipperary'; the silhouette of the speaker, with his passionate rhetoric, flashing intermittently through Act II; and the hypnotized rhythm of the speeches of the three young rebels at the end of Act II—all suggest strongly that O'Casey's technical experimentation began some while before his definite break with naturalism in Act II of *The Silver Tassie*."[41] It is the poet O'Casey, groping to find new techniques to convey his imaginative vision, who accounts for this burgeoning interest in scenic stylization, weird lighting, rhythmic dialogue-poetry, the abundance of music and song, and the pervasively ironic mood that engulfs the whole. Conversely, it is O'Casey, the realist, who provides the photographic vignettes of the Dublin streets, the dingy tenement interiors, and the censorious, acrid laughter that are present in the pub and looting scenes. The shifting temperamental inclinations of O'Casey again combine to produce another hybrid drama of caustic, sardonic comedy and ironic tragedy, of vision and verisimilitude.

THREE

DRAMAS OF CEREMONIAL RITUALISM AND SCENIC STYLIZATION

We do not want merely an excerpt from reality; it is the imaginative transformation of reality, as it is seen through the eyes of the poet, that we desire. The great art of the theatre is to suggest, not to tell openly; to dilate the mind by symbols, not by actual things; to express in Lear a world's sorrow, and in Hamlet the grief of humanity —O'Casey, *The Green Crow*

There is something of an old wive's tale in fine literature. The makers of it are like an old peasant telling stories of the great famine or the hangings of '98 or from his own memories. He has felt something in the depth of his mind and he wants to make it as visible and powerful to our senses as possible. He will use the most extravagant words or illustrations if they will suit his purpose. Or he will invent a wild parable, and the more his mind is on fire or the more creative it is, the less will he look at the outer world or value it for its own sake. It gives him metaphors and examples, and that is all.—W. B. Yeats, *Essays and Introductions*

Convinced that paralysis was general over all of Ireland—the clerics with their "mind-torturing catechism," the patriots with their frustration and frenzy over De Valera's pacification policy, the Abbey Theatre directors and players with their puritanism and censorship, and the labor leaders with their changed views, which had transformed Liberty Hall, the university of the Dublin workers, into a tomb—Sean O'Casey departed in 1926 from his native land—"a hall whose walls were roof-high stained-glass windows nationally designed"[1]—

to live in England, "feeling an urge of some hidden thing in him waiting its chance for an epiphany of creation."[2] Another Irishman had gone into exile.

Arriving in London, O'Casey was met by James B. Fagan, who worked tirelessly to acquaint him with both the men and milieu of the London theatrical world. O'Casey met the drama critics James Agate and Beverley Nichols and the playwright Arthur Pinero; he was made an honorary member of the fashionable Garrick Club; and he attended performances of a number of plays, including *Uncle Vanya*, *Easy Virtue*, *This Woman Business*, *Rose Marie*, and *Journey's End*, the later offering, in O'Casey's opinion, an incomplete, muted profile of war:

> Sherriff's *Journey's End*, which made of war a pleasant thing to see and feel; a strife put spiritually at a great distance; a demure echo, told under candlelight, at a gentle fireside, of a fight informal . . . the stench of blood hid in a mist of soft-sprayed perfume; the yells of agony modulated down to a sweet pianissimo of pain . . . all the mighty, bloodied vulgarity of war foreshortened into a petty, pleasing picture.[3]

So the London theatre of the 1920s both disappointed and disgusted the Irish newcomer. With its low pulsebeat, its falsity beneath jovial exteriors, its insipid dialogue, its facile resolutions, and its fidelity to the banality of surfaces, it was a drama of a false verisimilitude that often ignored the abrasive and sordid aspects of daily existence. What O'Casey, with his active, creative imagination, wanted was a more nonrepresentational drama that would dilate the mind by symbols—a drama that would transcend the four dismal walls of orthodox realism and project its vision in an exaggerated, even distorted, construct, a construct fusing icons, music, ritualized dance, incantation, song, and colorful tableaux into a dynamic pattern clearly designed to achieve intensity and novelty of effect. In short, he wanted an arresting new drama of abstract realism heightened by poetry, a new drama of Rabelaisian humor and quick transition from dance to debate; he wanted a new, schematicized, allegorical drama that would make subjective values —the internal world of hidden thought and impulse—concrete and colorful by means of various symbols.

The American Eugene O'Neill had experimented with a drama of distortion in *The Emperor Jones* (1920) and *The Hairy Ape* (1922)—expressionistic works of strange surrealism and syncopation focusing on psychic turbulence—and O'Casey hints that O'Neill's early atavistic studies may have had some impact upon his evolving concept of a flexible and fluid drama of intricate ceremonialism and ritualized rhythm:

> I certainly would not say I was greater than the great O'Neill; not even as great as he; certainly not his equal in philosophical thought. O'Neill is a giant of drama—American and the world. I have a special affection for 'The Hairy Ape' for it was praise of this play that gave me my first acquaintance with O'Neill. The great Irish labor leader, Jim Larkin (of whom Bernard Shaw said 'The greatest Irishman since Parnell'), back from an American visit, came to me in Liberty Hall, aglow with a play he had seen in New York—'The Hairy Ape.' 'Get the play, Sean, when it comes—a great work. This fellow, O'Neill, will do things in the theatre.' And by God, he did, even in this early roaring rebellious Caliban striking out blindly, but getting nowhere, save at the end to be crushed to death by his choice of a brother: a symbol of the then working class, divorced from decency, from charm, from culture. Different now; but bad enough, with millions still in the state of the Hairy Ape, which explains the Ed Sullivan shows on television with you there, with us here: pandering to the ignorant and dull-brained louts, worker and middle-class, bereft of any sense of music, art, or literature. O'Neill is like a great oak tree forever tussled about by a turbulent wind; and the 'Hairy Ape' was O'Neill's loud shout on a first advent to the drama.[4]

Yet O'Casey denies that he was profoundly influenced in his quest for the suitable dramatic design by any one particular playwright or play:

> Your first question (1): I wasn't 'triggered off' in any particular way, or by any particular influence; that is, in playwrighting.

> For better or worse, I am a blend of experience and absorption of the spirit in the old, old melodrama, which you never saw; of Shakespeare, and the Elizabethans; of Goldsmith, Sheridan, Shaw; with the insistent influence of the romantic poets, and of everything I read, including the Americans: Whitman, Jefferson, Emerson, Melville, Hawthorne, and Lincoln. In fact: a world of life is within me, and, I suppose, I have moulded it all into an O'Casey figure of color, line, form.[5]

The raw material of experience is moulded into an O'Caseyan figure of color, line, and form in the five dramas of O'Casey's middle period of extensive experimentation, works that reflect the dramatist's fascination with an art that gives more than a mere facsimile of life. *The Silver Tassie* (1928) records the physical and psychological disintegration of a superb athlete and hero-scapegoat, Harry Heegan, and is a modified passion play that fuses the Gregorian chant and the chalice with the chaos of war. *Within the Gates* (1933) is a dance-debate drama accenting the cynicism and sterility in Hyde Park, a twentieth-century wasteland in miniature. *The Star Turns Red* (1940) is a play of prophecy and revolution inspired by Jim Larkin's vision of a liberated proletariat. *Red Roses for Me* (1942) is a lyrical celebration of life and a portrait of a Dublin poet and laborer as a young man. And *Purple Dust* (1940) is a farcical exposure of a two-man English invasion of Ireland.

A Coal Vendor as Catalyst

It is *The Silver Tassie* that concerns us initially, and, in his autobiography, O'Casey identifies the human catalyst that ignited the creative process responsible for this play. The incident involved a casual, rewarding encounter with an unidentified London coal vendor—a portly man with a forceful personality and a love of laughter and song. Waiting in the coal company's cluttered office, O'Casey heard this large, gay vendor hum and then sing snatches of a song he had never heard before:

> Gae fetch to me a pint o' wine,
> An' full it in a sulver tossie;
> That I may drink before I gae
> A service tae my bonnie lossie.
>
> But it's no' the roar of sea or shore
> Wad mak' me langer wish tae tarry;
> Nor shout o' war that's heard afar—
> It's leavin' thee, my bonnie lossie.[6]

Startled, O'Casey could only assert that "Aaron's rod had budded."[7] In the days that followed, this "riotous and romantic song" remained in O'Casey's memory, and he hummed it as he meditated in his flat in South Kensington or walked down Cromwell Road.[8] O'Casey had experienced an epiphany in the grime and gloom of the vendor's office, and so he resolved to give the title of the song, "The Silver Tassie," to his next play.

Like *The Plough and the Stars*, this new play was to hold the mirror up to war, and yet it was to be dramaturgically different; the second act, for example, was to be an "impression" of war. O'Casey defines his objectives in this passage from his autobiography:

> He would set down without malice or portly platitude the shattered enterprise of life to be endured by many of those who, not understanding the bloodied melody of war, went forth to fight, to die, or to return again with tarnished bodies and complaining minds. He would show a wide expanse of war in the midst of timorous hope and overweening fear; amidst a galaxy of guns; silently show the garlanded horror of war. . . . The ruin, the squeal of the mangled, the softening moan of the badly rended are horrible, be the battle just or unjust; be the fighters striving for the good or manifesting faith in evil.[9]

Later the playwright remembers the difficulty he experienced in assembling the work, especially the second act, which is situated in the jagged and lacerated ruin of what was a monastery in the war zone somewhere in France:

> 'The Silver Tassie' was done easily in 1st Act, but the War Scene was a different problem. No one can put a war on the stage, even Shakespeare or the Soviet playwrights. I wished to give the spirit of the war, and to show the Christian fighters that [as] they slew and maimed each other before the face of the Son of God, tho' this idea was largely unconscious—it was how I seemed to feel; so, you may say, I drifted into it, because there was no other way. So I turned from 'realism,' tho' I'd written a one-act fantasy in 1926—*Kathleen Listens In*, and it was not new to me.[10]

O'Casey first gave the finished play to Sir Barry Jackson who quickly returned it, observing that the "terrible" play would excessively "lacerate" English feelings. Then William Butler Yeats objected to the work, insisting that O'Casey had no interest in the Great War: "You never stood on its battle fields or walked its hospitals, and so write out of your opinions."[11] Despite Yeats' reservations, O'Casey was confident that he had successfully captured the nightmarish dimensions of war. He had known soldiers since he was six. He had chatted with English Tommies in the hospitals of Saint Vincent and Richmond, and had "talked and walked and smoked and sung with the blue-suited, wounded men fresh from the front . . . the armless, the legless, the blind, the gassed, and the shell-shocked."[12] Like the American poet Walt Whitman, then, O'Casey relied upon his experience and his imaginative insight to guide him in his dramatic depiction of the red, roaring inferno of battle, his expressionistic vision of war.

And the vision that emerges from the grotesque verisimilitude in this work is an appalling one, reminding us anew that history is, as Stephen Dedalus argued, a nightmare from which we can't awaken; it is a recurring cycle of disagreements and

Heraclitean holocausts that leave the many twisted, embittered, and discarded veterans alone in the miasmatic meditations of their despairing thoughts. Confident that O'Casey's play had merit and undisturbed by the mushrooming controversy over the play's merits and defects, C. B. Cochran agreed to give *The Silver Tassie* a London première, and the artist Augustus John assisted with the kaleiodoscopic, surreal setting, silhouetting and juxtaposing the large, sinister gun and the colored church window in the Act II trench scene.[13]

SUBTLETY IN THE SCENARIO

Certainly it is the schematized stylization that is of special critical significance in this allegorical, ceremonial play, which focuses on Harry Heegan, the twenty-three-year-old splendid specimen and hero-victim whose tragic career suggests a duplication—perhaps a parody—of scapegoat rituals.[14] He is selected, honored, then rejected by the community, which turns then to a new hero, Heegan's companion, Barney Bagnal. Indeed, O'Casey's conscious and clear use of analogical alignments and recurring motifs—there is discernible duplication in the stage arrangements in the four acts, especially the first two—imparts to his play an organic unity, a tight continuity and cohesiveness reminiscent of early Strindbergian tragedy. Specifically, O'Casey uses his scenic similarities—the coherence in his evocative, pictorial configurations—to complement character transformation and transition, and to accentuate his bias about the alternating, cyclical nature of existence: life flows, then ebbs, only to flow again with different participants.

Acts I and II—the former situated in the eating-sitting-sleeping room of the Heegan House and the latter near a ruined monastery in the war zone somewhere in France—are, with some exceptions, strikingly similar, both assuming the aspect of a church or cathedral where a sacrifice is imminent. Both utilize large windows at the back, with the window in the first act looking out on a quay, and the window in the second looking out on a long expanse of denuded terrain disfigured by trenches, barbed wire, and stumps of trees. Visible through the first window is the center mast of a steamer with a gleaming white light at the top; visible through the second window is another cross formed by two broken pieces of masonry, one jutting from the left and another from the right. A white star glows above this wartime wasteland. Beneath and directly in front of the window in Act I is a stand with silver gilded top; the stand is flanked by a dresser to the left and a bed to the right, a pattern suggesting an altar and two pulpits. A purple velvet shield, to which are pinned a number of silver and gold medals, rests on the stand; two small vases containing artificial flowers stand on the two sides of the shield, a balanced grouping that again evokes an altar tableau. Directly in front of the window in Act II is a massive, black howitzer gun, emblematic of the weapons responsible for the maiming—the "crucifixion"—of Heegan, an action adumbrated by the symbolic mast-cross, altar-stand, and purple color of Act I. Significantly, the colors silver and gold are absent in the second act, since war—ugly trench war, killing thousands—is in the playwright's mind sans glory.

Other particulars reinforce the complementary nature of the two acts and remind us of the parallel patterns existing in both. In Act I Mrs. Heegan stands viewing the street through the right rear window; a right front door also provides access to the street. Hence both the window and the door provide Mrs. Heegan and others with means of escape from a house agitated at times by tension and turmoil. In Act II a stained-glass window containing a figure of the Virgin replaces Mrs. Heegan and her window while a life-sized crucifix replaces the front side street exit. A shell has blasted one arm from the cross and so the crucifix leans forward with the released arm outstretched towards the Virgin. In similar fashion, Harry Heegan, after having his legs immobilized, will later assume the attitude and posture of a suppliant before a crucifix-wearing Sister, a mortal virgin. As the people in Act I "escaped" through windows and doors, so do the soldiers seek escape and solace in religion in Act II. Ironically, the mother figures, Mrs. Heegan and Mrs. Foran, do not weep at the departure of their sons in Act I; in Act II, however, the Virgin Mother stares aghast and "white-faced" at the murder of many of her sons. The other passageway, the left bedroom door of Act I, becomes the Red Cross archway entrance in Act II, both entrances hinting at the peace that comes with rest, comfort, and security. Hence the location of doors and windows invites us to view the two settings as symbolically related.

Still other similarities integrate the two acts. Sylvester Heegan and Simon Norton, two dock workers, sit before a fire at middle left in Act I, reminiscing about Harry Heegan's past exploits with fists and feet, thereby identifying Heegan as a modern Oisin among the Avondales. In Act II a group of soldiers, wet, cold, and sullen-faced, form a circle at near center around a brazier in which a fire is burning. Since war is an ugly, deadly, larger game devoid of glory, they sing no songs to honor an Achilles in their midst but, rather, give us litanies of their profound grief and despair.

In Act I Sylvester and Simon must endure the doleful chanting—the "tambourine theology"—of Susie Monican, a religious fanatic who is momentarily obsessed with visions of man's innate depravity and the Last Judgment:

> Man walketh in a vain shadow, and disquieteth himself in vain:
> He heapeth up riches, and cannot tell who will gather them.[15]

In Act II the soldiers must listen to the Croucher, a blood- and mud-spattered soldier situated on a ramp above the brazier who sounds like Susie:

> And the hand of the Lord was upon me, and carried me out in the spirit of the Lord, and set me down in the midst of a valley.[16]

While Susie chanted of last things, so the Croucher intones dreamily of a valley of dry bones.

As she bombards the two men with the name of the deity, Susie, polishing a Lee-Enfield rifle, stands near a table at corner left on which are placed a bottle of whiskey, a large parcel of bread and meat sandwiches, and some copies of English illustrated magazines.[17] Near the table is a red-colored stand resembling an easel which holds a silver-gilt, framed picture of Harry Heegan in a crimson, yellow, and black football uniform. Susie's excessive concern with "everlastin'" fire and the rifle, the hero's iconlike portrait, the colors of violence (red and yellow), and the whiskey and sandwiches—perhaps connotations of the Eucharist here—again convey sacrificial overtones. In Act II Barney Bagnal, lashed to a gunwheel, replaces the picture of Heegan and the altar-table at left front. A soldier companion of Heegan, Barney is being punished for stealing a cock, hardly the kind of action one associates with a hero to be. Since Barney was an insignificant subordinate, an altar boy, in Heegan's Act I drink-dance, processional celebration—a Dionysian ballet pregnant with hints of disaster—it is appropriate that he be tied to but one of the several wheels of a large gun, the destructive instrument that will cripple Heegan for life.

It is quite significant that Heegan disappears in Act II and that Barney is given a promiment role in the action, for the process of transition from one hero to another is under way in this act. In Act I Barney was a doer, a coat-carrier, for the dynamic Harry; it was Heegan who won the gleaming tassie (the grail), the girl (Jessie Taite), and the glory (leading performer on the championship Avondale team). In Act II, however, Heegan is crippled while Barney remains uninjured and ready to assume Heegan's former heroic role; the alliteration in the two names suggests that O'Casey may have had this transference in mind. By Act IV Barney has gained the grail (twisted and bent), the girl (soiled but sentimental), and the glory (medals to attest to his bravery in battle), thereby completing the character-reversal pattern and strengthening the relationship among the acts.

A CRIPPLE AMONG CROSSES

Fewer scenic similarities are present in Acts III and IV, yet some continuity—scene linkage—is maintained. At the center rear in Act III, set in a hospital ward, is a large double door that opens onto a garden warmed by the rays of a setting September sun; at the center rear in Act IV, set in a room of the dance hall of the Avondale Football Club, is a wide, tall, window that also opens onto a garden. Three wooden crosspieces enabling weak patients to pull themselves into a sitting posture are attached to the beds at rear right in Act III; three black and red lanterns, with the center one four times the length of its width, form a corresponding illuminated cross at center front in Act IV. Situated before the large glass door in Act III is a white, glass-topped table on which rest medicines, drugs, and surgical instruments. The healing instruments of the surgeon have replaced the ugly, destructive howitzer of Act II. Also, a single vase of flowers, placed at the corner of the table, survives from the two that were on the altar-stand in Act I. No table is placed before the wide rear window in Act IV. Instead, a long table, covered with a green cloth and laden with bottles of wine and a dozen glasses, is situated at stage right. The concern for drinking and dancing has replaced the concern for healing, as music and vivid colors—gay festoons and colored streamers—have replaced the subdued tone and bleak austerity—the pervasive whiteness—of Act III. Significantly, the crucifix and the virgin have disappeared, the dancing couples preferring passionate self-indulgence to prayerful self-denial.

The characters also assume positions and reenact behavioral

patterns roughly analogous to those established in the previous two acts. In Act III Sylvester and Simon, in or near beds in the ward, perform a choral function as they comment again on hero Heegan—his crippled body and shattered dreams. In Act IV they first stand outside in the garden near the large, rear window, smoking and observing the activity at the dance; later they enter to sit before a fire to lament the reversal in the fortunes of Heegan, whose anguish is increased with the arrival of Barney, who leads Jessie Taite to the wine table as the act begins. As Harry's gold and silver medals adorned the purple shield in Act I, so now are war medals—one is ironically the Victoria Cross—attached to Bagnal's waistcoat. Barney had carried Heegan to safety in battle, but he now assists at his psychic disintegration. Likewise, as Harry and Jessie drank from the silver tassie in Act I, so now do Barney and Jessie drink from the wine glasses in this act.[18]

Also, Susie Monican, clad now in attractive, provocative attire, enters in Act III to again lecture Simon and Sylvester; however, she speaks no longer of sin and gloom but of sun, yellowing trees, and the active, joyful life. In Act IV she translates her doctrine into reality by dancing with surgeon Maxwell; she has completely reversed her previous pattern of thinking and acting. Finally, Mrs. Heegan no longer looks out of the window in Act IV; rather, she studies her embittered son through the doorway adorned with crimson and black curtains. Perhaps she has begun to manifest the charity so absent from the earlier acts. One new stage property—A Roll of Honour listing the names of the five members of the Avondale Club killed in battle—appears in Act IV at left back. A wreath of laurel tied with red and black ribbon rests underneath the Roll. As a symbolic epitaph, the Roll should also include Harry Heegan's name as he is "dead" in body and weakened in spirit. The others, responding to the gay fox trot and the bright future, represent a "full life on the flow"; Heegan, attended now by a new companion and follower, the blind

Teddy Foran, must be wheeled into the garden, a hulk of a man with his life on the ebb.[19]

As a ritualistic, carefully wrought passion play indicting the bloody butchery of war, *The Silver Tassie* possesses a subtle and pervasive unity distinguished by parallel patterns, interlocking triangles, ironic reversals, repetitive rhythms, and jagged but illuminating juxtapositions. Manipulating his recurring symbolic variables—windows, doors, tables, guns, photographs, icons, food, drink, lights, colors, and characters—O'Casey achieves a geometric consistency and symbolic density that some critics insisted were lacking in the earlier Dublin war plays. Commenting upon his ritual play thirty-one years after its London performance, O'Casey reiterates his major objectives:

> I wished to show the face and unveil the soul of war. I wanted a war play without noise; without the interruptions of gunfire, content to show its results, as in the chant of the wounded and the maiming of Harry; to show it in its main spiritual phases; its minor impulses and its actual horror of destroying the golden bodies of the young; and of the Church's damned approval in the sardonic hymn to the gun.[20]

Later, in another letter, of September 17, 1961, to this writer, O'Casey summarizes and applauds Robert Speight's critical response to the play:

> Yes, of course, you may use the quotation you mention. I don't mind the publication of anything I say or that I have said, provided that it is genuine—that my written name has been attached to it, and so made certain that it was said or written by me. Many things have been printed as said by me, things never said; many of them extraordinarily stupid that I couldnt think of saying; and one cant be always writing to contradict these things; so I am responsible only for those sayings and opinions which carry my name at the end—which, I believe, is fair to all.

> By the way, Robert Speight, the wellknown Eng. Actor (he was the creator of Becket in Eliot's MURDER IN THE CATHEDRAL), said of the TASSIE, in a letter defending it when it was violently denounced as blasphemous, etc, by the Irish clerics, that in this play O'Casey had snatched the veil from the hypocrisy and pretence of the Bourgeois, and had shown us all the true horror and blasphemy of war; and that christian killed and maimed christian under the clear view of Jesus, the Son of Man.
>
> He clearly saw the essence of the play.
>
> It is still a struggle to read or write, but I fight on, though I've been stuck fast to the bed for the last fortnight with a bout of bronchitis, but expect to be better soon.

Thus O'Casey had imposed an artist's pattern (his vision) upon war's pandemonium (a shell-blasted verisimilitude), fusing form and content in laudatory fashion and creating "a greater work than *The Plough and the Stars*."[21]

WITHIN THE GATES: THE MANIPULATION OF MYTH

Having emerged from *The Silver Tassie* controversy with increased confidence in his own talents, but with serious misgivings about the critical judgments of some of the directors of the Abbey Theatre, O'Casey next gave some thought to the possibility of preparing scripts for the movie industry. He had sold the movie rights to one of his earlier plays for a thousand pounds, money he needed desperately for his growing family, and he had discussed with Sydney Carroll, Adrian Brunel, Ivor Montague, Alfred Hitchcock, and others three embryonic ideas that he thought he could expand and adapt for cinematic utilization. One narrative was to focus on the career of Charles "Chinese" Gordon, the English explorer and soldier of fortune; another was to chronicle Ireland's saga, the

Cattle Raid of Cooley; and the third, which Hitchcock admired, was to concentrate upon the life that flowed through London's Hyde Park in one day:

> . . . a film of Hyde Park, London, its life, its color, its pathos, its pattern; its meaning to the rest of England. All its patterns to form a unity—its football, displays, speakers, evangelists, idlers, summer community singers; its swans, birds, dogs, traffic, and trees were to mingle together forming a changing and varied pattern around the life of a few people.[22]

O'Casey first gave the title "The Green Gates" to his Hyde Park pageant, a "geometrical and emotional" arrangement that was to begin with the opening of the park gates in the morning and end with the closing of the gates when Big Ben signalled the arrival of midnight. The pageant's four acts were to represent symbolically both the four seasons and the morning, noon, evening, and night cycle of one day. Moreover, each of the four divisions was to have its distinct color: a vivid green for the first, springtime act; crimson and gold for the noon segment; a crimson tinged with violet for the autumn interlude; and violet changing to purple and black in the last, bleak winter scene, these colors being the traditional liturgical colors of penance and death.[23]

Using judiciously selected, colorful details to convey a certain *vraisemblance*, O'Casey concentrates on his desired geometrical design, a design accenting the tangled network of relationships in the play. Integrating focal points of crisis, intersecting and overlapping lines of action, the beauty of certain angles in situations, and the ever-changing contours of figures in space, O'Casey, with admirable artistic calculation, gives us the geometry of near consummate art.

When Hitchcock failed to manifest further interest in O'Casey's Hyde Park scheme, O'Casey turned his back on the cinema and changed the title of his work to *Within the Gates*. Briefly, the drama records the frantic efforts of the Young

Woman—a voluptuous young female who is, as O'Casey says, too generous and sensitive to be a clever whore—to satisfy her physical needs and spiritual longings amidst a motley of amoral London residents distinguished by greed, cynicism, and despairing complacency.[24] Abandoned by her father, the Bishop; abused by her drunken mother, the Old Woman; raised by nuns, who terrify her with Dantean descriptions of the agonies of hell; and turned out by the Atheist, the Young Woman, named Jannice, finally takes to the streets (like Stephen Crane's Maggie) in order to earn money and to find freedom and some affection. Exploited by a number of lustful, egocentric males and sneered at by envious, self-righteous women, she momentarily subscribes to the Dreamer's vision of courageous, joyful life. Ultimately, however, she succumbs to the theology of the Bishop and dies making the sign of the cross. Numerous other figures—Chair Attendants, the Atheist, the Evangelists, Nursemaids, a Gardener, and the Salvation Army Officer, to cite but a few—swarm through this modern morality play.[25]

In arranging this choral drama, this allegory of post-World War I economic depression and spiritual disenchantment,[26] O'Casey introduced and integrated a technical innovation into his expanding dramatic design, resorting to the deliberate use of the mythical method that contrasted modern England with ancient Greece and Rome. O'Casey's countryman Joyce had utilized this method in a systematic and successful fashion in his *Ulysses* (1922), counterpointing twentieth-century Ireland and ancient Greece, and T. S. Eliot, recognizing Joyce's significant achievement, predicted that other modern writers would appropriate the mythical method as a means of providing scaffolding for their various fictions:

> In using the myth, in manipulating a continuous parallel between contemporaneity and antiquity, Mr. Joyce is pursuing a method which others must pursue after him. They will not

> be imitators, any more than the student who uses the discoveries of an Einstein in pursuing his own, independent, further investigation. It is simply a way of controlling, of ordering, of giving a shape and a significance to the immense panorama of futility and anarchy which is contemporary history. . . . Instead of narrative method, we may now use the mythical method.[27]

Eliot had himself utilized the mythical method in "The Waste Land," also published in 1922, to illuminate the inertia and spiritual indifference of contemporary society. Profoundly influenced by Jessie Weston's *From Ritual to Romance* (1920), Eliot had discovered a recurrent pattern of similarity in numerous myths, including various vegetation and fertility rituals, and the Christian versions of the Easter resurrection and the Grail legend. By weaving these ancient myths into his poems about London, Eliot was able to suggest something about the sameness—the basic continuity—of human experience. As F. O. Matthiessen observes: "The poem thus embodies simultaneously several different planes of experience, for it suggests the likeness between various waste lands. Its quest for salvation in contemporary London is given greater volume and urgency by the additional presence of the haunted realm of medieval legend."[28] Hence myths provided Eliot with the scaffold that enabled him to impart coherence to his diversified data and to comment upon the multiplicity of the modern, myth-minded world.

Now twelve years after the appearance of *Ulysses* and "The Waste Land" in 1922, O'Casey was to experiment with the mythical method, with the archetypal patterns of earlier Christian and pre-Christian literature in his ambitious drama of modified Expressionism, a work in which a series of vignettes of futility are fused into another waste land—the modern city of despair, decay, and death. And it is in the steadily changing landscape that we find the most strikingly apparent affinity between O'Casey's drama and the vegetation myths concerned with the fundamental rhythm of nature, because the four scenes in *Within the Gates* are obviously intended to reflect the cycle of the seasons, the rebirth and death of the year.

Scene I takes place in the park on a spring morning as birds build nests, fowl swim in the lake, and buds expand on the dark brown branches of trees. A chorus of young boys and girls, representing trees and flowers, enters to sing "Our Mother the Earth is a Maiden Again." A sexual union is suggested as the Earth Maiden seeks out her bridegroom, the Sun, in the "lovely confusion" of birds, blossoms, and buds. The chorus asserts that the Earth as Maiden "hears a challenge to life and to death as she dances along."[29] We are at high noon in summer in Scene II, and the colors are mainly golden glows; the green in the park sward is tinted with a golden yellow that hints at the approaching decay. It is an autumn evening in Scene III, and the leaves, some of them falling, are red and yellow. The few sunflowers are tall and gaunt, withering stalks of beauty. Finally, it is a winter night in Scene IV, and the trees are quite bare, their branches forming strange patterns against the purple parts of the sky.

JANNICE: DUALITY IN A DANCER

Appropriately, it is the Young Woman who is central to the fertility motif in *Within the Gates*, because her function seems to be the restoration of potency, both physical and spiritual, to the dying park and its confused members. Indeed, her role seems multidimensional and, at times, self-contradictory. Her name, Jannice, quickly identifies her with Janus, the Roman god of doorways and the special patron of all new undertakings. As the god of beginnings, Janus' blessing was sought at the beginning of each day, month, and year, and at all births, the beginning of life. Jannice is, therefore, O'Casey's guardian of the park gates, and is the fair maid referred to in the song celebrating the arrival of spring in Scene I. She is also largely responsible for a birth—the proud Bishop's birth into a new humility and a compassionate awareness, which occurs at the play's close. (Additional discussion of the Bishop's transformation will come later.)

Jannice resembles her two-faced Roman namesake in still another way: a duality in her nature causes her to behave like a fertility goddess at one moment, like a questing Christian seeking salvation, the next. As a fertility figure, Jannice is associated in a muted fashion with Diana, the young Roman goddess of noble beauty, who was guardian of flocks and fields. Although Diana was regarded as the chaste goddess of the hunt, Sir James G. Frazer suggests in *The Golden Bough* that she emerged from earlier, more primitive fertility figures in ancient vegetation ceremonies. Thus Diana, "as goddess of nature in general, and of fertility in particular," also came to be regarded as "a personification of the teeming life of nature, both animal and vegetable."[30] Although Diana was frequently depicted with a bow, quiver, and javelin, she was also sometimes identified with a crescent.[31] It is not accidental, therefore, that O'Casey repeatedly stresses the fact that his Jannice has a black crescent on her hat and a scarlet one on her hip. Jannice's mother, for example, mentions this fact twice in Scene IV. Moreover, the Dreamer reinforces this woman-nature motif in Scene II when he likens Jannice's legs to the fresh, golden branches of a willow and her breasts to gay, white apple blossoms.

As a fertility figure, Jannice is eagerly sought after by virtually all the males in the park, but especially by the Gardener, a hedonistic opportunist who sings of folding a girl in his arms. As Frazer observes, "it behooved Diana to have a male partner" if she were to be fruitful.[32] It is the Gardener's singing that prompts the crowd of couples to sing of Adam discovering Eve, with her "beauty" shining through a "mist of golden hair." Notice also that it is the Gardener who carries the black maypole, an ancient phallic symbol, which is later used in the folk dancing designed to make England "merry again."[33] Moreover, it is the Man with the Stick who in Scene I lectures the Gardener about the maypole as "symbol," informing him, "It represents life, new life about to be born; fertility; th' urge wot was in the young lass [Jannice]."[34] Finally, it is appropriate for the young boys and girls dancing around the maypole to sing the folk song "Haste to the Wedding," because Jannice repeatedly insists that marriage, a home, and children mean "everything to me, everything."[35]

As indicated, Jannice also seems at times to take on additional shadowy dimensions that link her with the questing Christian, especially the courageous knight of medieval romance who sought the Fisher King's castle so that he could lift the curse from the parched land, purifying himself in the process. When O'Casey first introduces Jannice, he states that she has a "preoccupied and rather anxious look on her face, and appears to be searching for someone."[36] Ironically, hers is the archetypal quest for a spiritual father who is also her biological father. Like the male knight of earlier romance, Jannice, too, has her courage severely tested by the arguments of the Atheist, the hatred of the Bishop's sister, the attempted seductions by various males, the hypocritical, evangelical fervor of the Salvation Army Officer, and the physical abuse of the Old Woman. She perseveres, however, persistently maintaining that her dancing and song are better for man's health and salvation than the doleful chant of the Down-and-Out.

Jannice ultimately confronts the Bishop, the pompous cleric, and compels him in a heated debate (perhaps a reversal of the knight's ritual interrogation) to see himself and his religion in a new light. In her final moments, Jannice also recognizes her own imperfections, admitting that she has "a lot to answer for."[37] The Bishop indicates, however, that she, like the questing knight, has cleansed herself through suffering, when he declares that God will "find room for one scarlet blossom among a thousand white lilies."[38]

The Bishop as Sick Fisher King

If Jannice resembles, in part, the Christian knight struggling for salvation, the Bishop has much in common with the sick Fisher King, for he is the figure of authority in the decaying park crowded with the living dead largely devoid of hope and charity. The Bishop, a man of sixty or so, has lost much of his physical vitality and, as O'Casey points out, his powers "are beginning to fail."[39] However, his real sickness is spiritual. All his life he has, like Hawthorne's Puritan divine, lived a lie, refusing to admit that he, as a young theology student, seduced a pretty housemaid and later abandoned both mother and child. He later compounded his sin by refusing to involve himself in the vital work of the church, much of it concerning church members from a lower social stratum.

As he himself admits, his "besetting sin" was a fear of the opinions of his respectable parishioners; like his harsh sister, he fled from "the sour touch of common humanity."[40] As a timid, class-conscious clergyman preaching the gospel of complacency, the Bishop is therefore largely responsible for the spiritual aridity of the park. His ineptness helped to create the prevalent cynicism and atheism and to produce the pessimistic attitudes of the Down-and-Out, hopeless specimens who carry the "fainting flag" of a dead faith and live a life of meek obedience and resignation. Their slogan is "Welcome to the Will of God" and he calls them "God's Aristocracy." Through his contact with the Young Woman, however, the Bishop is given a second chance. He confesses that by trying to save his "honoured soul," he may have lost it, and he directs his astonished sister to go home and ask God's mercy on all of them. Hence, Jannice has helped to heal him of the sins of pride and complacency, and the drama's ending suggests that the curse may be lifted from the bleak park: "The sky's purple and black changes to a bright grey, pierced with golden segments, as if the sun was rising, and a new day about to begin."[41]

With the coming of a new age, the confused people in the park may turn with renewed hope to the revitalized Bishop, rejecting the War Memorial Figure, a massive monument that towers above the park like a menacing, indifferent, demonic deity—a god of war. In Scene I O'Casey describes this steel-helmeted soldier as having a bent head and "skeleton-like hands" holding a rifle. He wears a hat with a wide circle, suggestive of a halo. With his sharp, angular lines, he seems to be "shrinking back" from the new life that is emerging. Late in Scene II and Scene III O'Casey likens the soldier to a giant clad in gleaming steel or burnished aluminum. It is in the last scene that the Old Woman brings a wreath to the Memorial, lifting it high above her head like a priest "elevating the Host"; she refers to the soldier as the cold guard of remembrance for those who fell in battles, especially her husband, the Irish Dragoon. If the Young Woman stands for the love and personal energy that produce and sustain new life, the soldier represents the opposite—the hate and impersonal violence that shatter vital young men.[42]

Discussing the unique structural synthesis that he sought to achieve in *Within the Gates*, O'Casey revealed that he had attempted to fuse qualities from classical, romantic, and expressionistic plays into a "new" form. Rejecting the fake verisimilitude—the "dead naturalism"—that had stripped the drama of his day of its beauty, intensity, and poetry, O'Casey defended his vision of a "dancing" drama that would blend fantasy, music, song, dance, and splendor of scene into carefully wrought patterns: "*Within the Gates* tries to bring back to the drama the music and song and dance of the Elizabethan play and the austere ritual of the Greek drama, caught up and blended with the life around us."[43] Hence it was the timeless patterns of myth (especially pagan)—with their suggestions of life renewed after arduous struggle—that enabled O'Casey, like his gifted countryman James Joyce, to throw into high, sharp relief both the paralysis and the potential of another wasteland—of a microcosm with abandoned child, remorseful father, and wandering bard.

O'Casey's idiosyncratic vision affects drastically the detailed but revelatory verisimilitude in this somber pageant: indeed, we have a fusion that results in visionary verisimilitude. In the many intricately interrelated episodes in this drama of experimental mythology, the concrete details radiate layers of meaning, existing as both physical objects in themselves and as symbolic variables pointing to larger implications. The dying park is irradiated at intervals with gleams of hope as O'Casey successfully achieves the concrete visualization of the moods of the major figures, especially Jannice.

PURPLE DUST: JOHN BULL AND HIS OTHER ISLAND

> The winds of change come, and no one feels them till they become strong enough to sweep things away, carrying men and women (however comic and enjoyable), bearing off their old customs, manners, and morals with them. . . . There are those who clutch at things that are departing, and try to hold them back. . . . They try to shelter from the winds of change but Time wears away the roof, and Time's river eventually sweeps the purple dust away.—O'Casey, *Under a Colored Cap*

O'Casey deliberately exaggerates the contrast, the great disparity, between the discontented and divided present and the reconciled and united future in two of his protest plays that follow *Within the Gates*, two plays of hopeful prognostication that focus on the political-economic polarities that cause strikes and revolutions. The established, reactionary church and state are displaced in *The Star Turns Red*, and the play concludes with O'Casey's visionary depiction of the arrival of a workers' democracy, a vision illuminated by a glowing red star and enlivened by the exultant insurgents' singing of "The Internationale." In *Red Roses for Me*, O'Casey first depicts Dublin as a "bleak, black, and bitter" city, a city of "poverty, penance, and pain" where the outer gloom and drabness equals and emphasizes the inner despair of its inhabitants. Then, in Act III, this drab Dublin, caught in the golden rays of an extraordinary sunset, is transformed into a city of joy and splendor, the visionary embodiment of poet-proletarian Ayamonn Breydon's dream of a liberated Ireland, of a utopia of the future sans poverty and pessimism. It is a many-splendored vision, a colorful panorama of the future, as the people, some of them clad in gay garments, sing and then dance before buildings that glow in the light. Vision transforms verisimilitude in this version of Ayamonn's dream that manipulates Irish myth, measuring the Irishmen of the present against the legendary heroes of the past: Finn Mac Cool, Brian Boru, Goll Mac Morna, and Oscar.

Yet the needle of O'Casey's creative compass, never at rest, subsequently veered away from violent social upheaval to point in *Purple Dust* toward a different locale, toward a different reality, often more farcical than fractious—the reality of tangled English-Irish relationships. Numerous other writers before O'Casey had tapped this vein of rich ore, and if one arbitrarily selects Jonathan Swift's "A Modest Proposal" (1729) as a recognizable point of departure, one can quickly compile an impressive list of subsequent works, many of them dramatic, that investigate Anglo-Irish relationships, especially those situations—amorous, ecclesiastical, and economic—that are pregnant with satirical potential. In 1761 George Coleman includes an Irish adventurer, Captain O'Cutter, in his cast of English country squires, unprincipled aristocrats, and virile city men in *The Jealous Wife*. Richard Cumberland follows with *The West Indian* (1771), which studies the kindly Irishman Major O'Flaherty and the sanctimonious English woman Lady Rusport. Richard Brinsley Sheridan satirizes the Irish gallant Sir Lucius O'Trigger and the country squire Bob Acres in *The Rivals* (1775), an expose of the absurdity of the heroic code; additional Irish "types" appear in his *St. Patrick's Day*, a short farce written in the same year. Thomas Moore reminds the "faithless sons" of Erin that the emerald gem must be removed from the "crown of a stranger" in his nationalistic *Irish Melodies* (1807–1835). In *The Green Bushes* (1845), the Victorian writer J. B. Buckstone adds to the emerging pattern with his hero, Connor O'Kennedy, who, fearful of arrest, flees Ireland to consort with a motley of Americans and Europeans. William Makepeace Thackeray gives us the autobiography of an Irish rogue in *The Luck of Barry Lyndon, Esq*. (1884), and Tennyson's friend, Aubrey de Vere, reveals his Irish bias in "English Misrule and Irish Misdeeds" (1848). Dion Boucicault exploits Anglo-Irish antagonism in his melodramatic *Arrah-na-Pogue* (1864) and *The Shaughraun* (1875), the former recording the escape of an Irish rebel leader from the British. Seumas O'Kelley, Daniel Corkery, and Liam O'Flaherty concentrate upon the frustrations and chaotic violence that attended Ireland's confused struggle for independence in *The Parnellite* (1917), *The Hounds of Banba* (1920), and *The Informer* (1925). Sean O'Faolain and Iris Murdoch tap the same vein and bring the Anglo-Irish tradition into the midtwentieth century in *Midsummer Night Madness* (1932) and *The Red and the Green* (1965), the latter a novel of the 1916 Easter Week rebellion.

As dramas dealing with Anglo-Irish confrontations, *Purple Dust*, a poetic farce fusing the mundane and the mysterious, and George Bernard Shaw's *John Bull's Other Island* (1904), a play written at Yeats' instigation as an offering to the Irish literary theatre, must be added to this incomplete list, and the two satirical studies are strikingly similar in some respects, especially in the basic plot situations.[44]

Briefly, both dramas study English expeditions to Ireland. *John Bull's Other Island* chronicles the varied adventures of Thomas Broadbent and Laurence Doyle, civil engineers representing an English land development syndicate, as they devise and execute plans to transform Rosscullen, a minor hell of monotony, bigotry, and hopelessness, into the Garden City of Ireland—into a flourishing resort area with hotel, golf links, art center, polytechnic school, library, and modernized transportation, including a light railway and motor boats. This ambitious commercial venture seems destined to succeed because Broadbent, pragmatic senior partner in the firm, eventually wins the respect of the Irish farmers, who want him to represent them in Parliament; the approbation of the local clergy—no small feat—and the hand of an Irish maiden Nora Reilly, Doyle's former sweetheart. The play ends as Broadbent and Doyle move off to select an appropriate site for the new hotel.

O'Casey's *Purple Dust* likewise focuses on two affluent Englishmen, Cyril Poges and Basil Stoke, who attempt to refurbish a decayed Tudor-Elizabethan mansion in Clune na Geera so that they, as cavalier country gentlemen, may experience the energy, imagination, and hilarity of a vanished age and the therapeutic benefits of nature. Material considerations are not completely abandoned, however, since both Englishmen hope that, with the acquisition of livestock (hens and cows), the estate will become self-supporting. The pertinacity and crafty ebullience of the intractable Irish workers, which cause several *mésaventures;* the amoral opportunism of the Irish mistresses, Souhaun and Avril, who desert their English benefactors in their hour of peril; and the fury of the elements—a flood engulfs the house in the final scene—all combine to shatter the Englishmen's epic dream. The play ends with

Poges' importunate pleading for a return to sane, secure England. So they shout an elegy in an Irish countryside.

The Victims of Change

These plays reflect their authors' disgust with extravagant, fraudulent sentiment, their sensitivity to suffering, their awareness of class antagonisms, and, to some extent, their contempt for tradition. It is, however, the exposure of the madness, spiritual torpidity, and economic stagnation that invariably follow when people develop a paralyzing preoccupation with the remote and the illusory that emerges as the major objective of both works. Excessive, neurotic fascination with the imaginatively rehearsed splendors of the past makes people—so Shaw and O'Casey suggest—inept participants in the present, rendering them victims and enemies of change, innovation, and progress.[45]

Numerous scenes in the two plays articulate this thesis. In Act I of *John Bull's Other Island*, Doyle thanks his English partner for training him (Larry) "to live in a real world and not in an imaginary one."[46] With curt sincerity Larry later informs his ex-sweetheart, Nora, that her future life with Broadbent will mean "no more neglect, no more loneliness, no more idle regrettings and vain-hopings in the evenings by the round tower, but real life and real work and real cares and real joys among real people."[47] In Act IV he again expresses the hope that the systematic English Land Syndicate, with its "gospel of efficiency," will "grind the nonsense" out of, and some "strength and sense" into, the Irish, especially the youth of Ireland.

In a somewhat similar scene in Act I of *Purple Dust*, O'Killigain, supervisor of the Irish workers repairing the mansion, refuses to share Poges' fondness for "great things past," the young Irish worker affirming that "life as it is, and will be, moves me more."[48] Later in a heated exchange in Act II, O'Killigain asks the stunned Poges:

> Why don't you seek to build a house that will give a royal chance of bringing newer skill and a newer idea of life to the men who build it? Why don't you try to bring newer grace and form and line before the eyes of Clune na Geera? Why th' hell don't you try to do something worthwhile?[49]

Still later, O'Killigain, who could well be speaking for both playwrights, insists that time, money, and energy should only be expended "in building something new, something showing a new idea, leading our eyes to the future."[50]

If the basic themes are similar, the dramatic techniques are not. Shaw concentrates on the contrast between two relatively intelligent people and a society dominated by primitive conservatives who are often both gross and greedy. Broadbent, with some assistance from Doyle, is the character who stands for the sanity of Shavian pragmatism and progress; it is he who thinks in terms of machinery, employment opportunities, and material utility in a frequently ridiculous, impoverished, and convention-shackled world. Broadbent is not, however, a perfect paradigm who escapes Shaw's raillery; this gullible, "conquering Englishman's" farcical conduct and sentimental excesses (Shaw contends that a sentimental Englishman is like a drunk Irishman) help diminish his success. Like Swift and Joyce, then, Shaw displays an ambivalent attitude toward his hero and numerous other major figures; he alternately applauds and criticizes his characters, thereby creating an ironic situation that is intricate and sometimes self-contradictory.[51]

O'Casey, on the other hand, follows the conventional formula employed by most satiric dramatists. He juxtaposes two fatuous characters, distinguished by comic rigidity and varying degrees of irrationality, with a society that displays a fair amount of moderation and mobility. The absurd scheme to reclaim a worm-eaten mansion near a river that consistently overflows its banks identifies Poges and Stoke as two romantic dolts with limited vision—as two impractical creatures who deserve to be exploited by sensible, shrewd Irish bucolics. Hence O'Casey's comedy lacks the infinite complexities of irony—both of statement and situation—that enhance Shaw's play because O'Casey's characters retain an easily perceived, fixed value. One looks in vain for the elusive, multidimensional personality in *Purple Dust*. One finds, instead, two categories of unidimensional people: the clever Irish and the foolish English.

PRAGMATIC DREAMERS AND TWO FOOLS

There are some superficial similarities in the character and conduct of the two senior members in the two partnerships. Both Broadbent, a robust, Gladstonized Englishman in the prime of his life, and Poges, a stout old fellow of sixty-five who likes to intimidate by bluster, are secular evangelists fond of delivering soporific sermons on the glories of English capital, knowledge, and resourcefulness—the "gospel of efficiency." Defenders of English colonialism, both believe that England has an obligation to place her capacity for government at the service of less fortunate nations. As the prolix Poges declares: "Wherever we have gone, progress, civilization, truth, justice, honour, humanity, righteousness, and peace have followed at our heels."[52] Handicapped by some naïve, stereotyped notions about the charm and wit of the Irish, both men are also fond of regarding themselves as sensible, unemotional Englishmen capable of living the "solid four square life." Hence Broadbent emerges as a romantic realist—an idiot and a genius as Doyle states it—who is clever in his foolishness. Enormously absurd in his solemn, self-conscious moments, Broadbent is, nevertheless, a shrewd man who "muddles through" to successful achievement. Poges is less of a genius and more of an idiot—a romantic idiot at that. Lacking Broadbent's balance and common sense, he is a marplot overly fond of paraphrasing Wordsworth, misquoting other poets, and using historical illustrations tendentiously. Souhaun's description of him as a "dim-eyed, half-dead, old fool" is most apt.

There are fewer affinities to be noted in the careers of the junior partners in the two alliances. Doyle, a clever, handsome, Anglicized Irishman in his midthirties, is a realistic romantic like Shaw (whom he greatly resembles); he hates maudlin men and economic bleakness, broods about the tragedies of wasted youth and stunted minds, and longs for a country where "the facts were not brutal and the dreams not unreal."[53] Anxious to see the Irish Catholic Church above worldly pride and ambition, and the Irish nation as the "brains and imagination of a big commonwealth," the pragmatic Doyle is nevertheless fully cognizant of the great charm and hypnotic power of the dream. Speaking for himself and virtually all other sensitive, intelligent Irishmen, Doyle comments at length on the antagonism between the ideal and the real, and the problems created by the Irishman's imagination, in this illuminating speech from Act I:

> An Irishman's imagination never lets him alone, never convinces him, never satisfies him, but it makes him that he cant face reality nor deal with it nor handle it nor conquer it. . . . And all the time you laugh, laugh, laugh! eternal derision, eternal envy, eternal folly, eternal fouling, staining and degrading, until, when you come at last to a country where men take a question seriously and give a serious answer to it, you deride them for having no sense of humor, and plume yourself on your own worthlessness as if it made you better than them.[54]

With his insight and sensitivity, Doyle affords a strong contrast with Basil Stoke, a long, thin, fatuous man of thirty with a gloomy face. A pompous philosopher who has "passed" through Oxford, Stoke likes to boast of his knowledge of Aristotle, Plato, Locke, Kant, Spinoza, and others, stoutly maintaining that all people should have "ready respect and veneration" for scholars. Possessing abundant knowledge but little wisdom, Stoke consistently displays hauteur in his dealings with the Irish rustics, even with Avril, his pert and pretty mistress. Excessive rigidity and pride combine to make Stoke a ludicrous figure, and we delight in his humiliation at the play's close.

Sentimentality and Sanity among Women and Priests

The women are likewise creatures of contrast. Shaw's Nora Reilly is a slight, weak, sentimental young woman with little knowledge of life outside Rosscullen. A believer in the fiction of romantic love and pure, indissoluble marriage, she, as a typical Shavian womanly woman, has waited eighteen years for the return of her childhood sweetheart, Doyle, who now views her as a helpless, useless, almost sexless creature, as an "incarnation of everything in Ireland that drove him out of it."[55] When Larry jolts her pride with jest and insult and reduces her to tears with his blunt critical remarks, she turns to Broadbent, who finds her an attractive, charming woman. Her future life with this prospective Member of Parliament promises to liberate her from the drabness and dullness of village life, affording her, as Broadbent asserts, "comfort and common sense—and plenty of affection."[56]

O'Casey's Souhaun, a good-looking woman of thirty-two,

and Avril, a pretty girl of twenty-one very much aware of her good looks, are emancipated, voluptuous, scheming women with a knowledge of men and affairs. Both regard their benefactors with contempt, Souhaun persistently referring to Poges as an "old fool," and Avril calling Stoke a "perjurer in passion." They flatter and deceive their English lovers to gain certain creature comforts—modern conveniences, petty cash, and attractive wardrobes—and they finally achieve financial independence when the two Englishmen settle five hundred pounds a year on each of them for life. In the end they desert Poges and Stoke to join "firm-fed men and comely, cordial women" where there is "laughter round a red fire."[57]

Unlike the women, the priests in both plays have much in common. Shaw's Father Dempsey and O'Casey's Canon Creehewel are both conservative, money-conscious clerics with respect for tradition. Father Dempsey is hostile to scientific skepticism and new theories in general (i.e., the notion that the round towers are phallic symbols), while Canon Creehewel fears the "present swirl of young life" and the sexual desires of men and women. Father Dempsey is, quite clearly, the stronger of the two, taxing his flock severely and insisting that they fully recognize his authority. Creehewel is more an apologetic peddler of platitudes. It is the "mad" ex-priest Peter Keegan who emerges as the individual with the most insight into spiritual realities.[58] A visionary with the face of a young saint who is tortured by his dreams of perfection, Keegan, like William Blake, believes that all that lives is holy and regards this earth as a place of torment where the fool is rewarded and the wise man neglected and abused. (His conversation with the grasshopper in the beginning of Act II reminds one of the Caesar's chat with the sphinx in *Caesar and Cleopatra*.) He dislikes the Englishmen's "foolish dream of efficiency" that will transform the Isle of the Saints into a busy mint where the Irish will slave to make money for the Syndicate, but he knows that it will succeed because the Englishman is "clever in his foolishness" while the Irishman is merely "foolish in his cleverness." He finally concedes, however, that the Irish, who do nothing, have no right to sneer at the English, who at least do something. Hence he indicates that he will probably vote for Broadbent, realizing that an efficient man who knows his mind and business is better by far than a foolish patriot. However, he refuses to discard his dream of a country where "work would be play and play life," and we last see him moving up the hill toward the round tower to dream of heaven.

A Poet and Some Yahoos

There are no characters in *Purple Dust* like Shaw's "mad" priest, but Philib O'Dempsey, an O'Killigain associate fecund of observation and comment, resembles Keegan with his fondness for dreams, the good, free life, and Ireland's scenic beauty. His persiflage with Souhaun, whom he finally wins, accounts for much of the play's poetry. Aside from O'Killigain, who obviously represents the sound sense of O'Caseyan practicality and progress and who wins Avril's affections, the other Irish workers are not carefully delineated. Sensible and shrewd, they provide satiric, choral commentary upon the action while attempting, along with some Irish farmers, to exploit the English visitors. Shaw's rustics are not carefully differentiated either, most of them emerging as typical Shavian philistines—as unsophisticated fellows who rejoice in material possessions and pursue self-interests. Tim Haffigan is an impoverished rascal overly fond of drink and eloquence; Patsy Farrell is both callow and cunning; Barney Doran is intolerant and impulsive, a lover of cruel, obscene jokes; Cornelius Doyle, Larry's father, is conservative and materialistic; and Matt Haffigan is an ignorant Irishman with a quick temper. The essential difference, therefore, between the two groups of laborers is that O'Casey's are clever and Shaw's are crude.

These two groups of rowdy rustics are given prominent roles in the low-comedy scenes, most of which occur in *Purple Dust*. The one riotous episode in *John Bull's Other Island* occurs when Broadbent attempts to transport a pig to Matthew Haffigan's farm, a wild ride that shatters Molly Ryan's crockery stall, the village market, and other Rosscullen structures. When Cornelius Doyle argues that this public disaster will jeopardize Broadbent's chances for a seat in Parliament, Larry disagrees, asserting that Broadbent will "never know theyre laughing at him; and while theyre laughing he'll win the seat."[59] While Shaw's farcical episode provides additional insight into English and Irish character, many of O'Casey's mishaps seem to be farcical situations in and for themselves. For example, the smashing of the ceiling by the Yellow-Bearded Man in Act I, the shattering of a wall by Poges and his giant lawn roller, the shooting of a harmless cow by Stoke in Act II, and the abusing of a door and the quattrocento chest by Poges and the workers in Act III enliven the play, but contribute little that is new or unusual in the way of character revelation. Hence *John Bull's Other Island* is essentially a Shavian discussion drama, an overly long, sustained cerebral orchestration, while *Purple Dust* frequently approaches farce, repeatedly relying on cardboard characters who romp through stock situations merely for the sake of the action itself.

EXPRESSIONISTIC ELEMENTS IMPART DIMENSION

Yet O'Casey is more of a poet in *Purple Dust* than Shaw is in his play—more of an artist determined to accent his satiric paradigm with new terms and techniques minted in the creative forge of his private sensibility. Hence O'Casey resorts to the use of symbolic characters, costumes, properties, and settings. Near the end of *Purple Dust* he introduces, amidst flickering lightning, the Figure, an ominous, hooded man with a blue mask and gleaming black oilskins, to represent the spirit of the turbulent waters. His minatory utterances adumbrate the play's crisis. The Yellow-Bearded Man and the Postmaster are other semisymbolic figures reminiscent of certain characters in O'Casey's earlier dramas of modified Expressionism, *The Silver Tassie* and *Within the Gates*. The symbolic clothing and properties appear early in Act I when the Englishmen, their mistresses, and their Irish servants engage in an absurd "country style" dance. Each dancer wears a smock with a stylized animal on the front and carries a farm implement that serves to illuminate his personality. As an obese, aging Casanova, Poges fittingly carries a wooden rake and a pig's picture. While long-winded Stoke carries a spade and a hen's picture, matronly Souhaun is identified with a cow and a hoe, and energetic, pleasure-loving Avril, a garland of daisies around her neck, is adorned with a duck and a shepherd's crook. In addition, the interior of the ancient mansion is cleverly arranged so as to resemble a "gigantic cage."

O'Casey also imparts an intriguing dimension to his drama through the use of mythical motifs: the coming of the floods and the reawakening of new life in spring. The swirling new waters wash away the old, forcing Poges to retreat into the temporary security of his quattrocento chest (his closing of the lid above his head reminds one of death and the disappearance of a victim into a coffin). Coming in April, these waters simultaneously offer promise of a glorious rebirth of vigorous life in the spring. Appropriately, Avril (April) is referred to as a "sweet bud" of an "out-spreading tree," and O'Killigain's invitation to her to join him "where the rain is heavy . . . and . . . the sun warm," and where love is "fierce an' fond an' fruitful" indicates that the blasted rowan tree, identified in Act I as the symbol of life through love, may again flourish and produce red berries. Indeed, O'Casey declares that the new blossoms will "form a bridal veil."

Strategically spaced off-stage sounds contribute significantly to the larger rhythmic variations in *Purple Dust*. Frequently these sounds operate as an ironic counterpoint to the dialogue, undercutting and punctuating the pompous, unrealistic utterances of the two Englishmen and Canon Creehewel with hints of impending disaster. For example, when the Canon rails in Act III about O'Killigain as the snake in the Irish Eden, wind and rain batter the old house. Poges' long second-act discourse on the dignity of old houses is interrupted with the ominous sounds of falling rain and peals of thunder. The sounds of trotting horses and crowing cocks recur continually, lending emphasis to the cuckoldry motif, since it is on wild horses that the young Irishmen eventually flee with Souhaun and Avril. It is this natural world of great energy and unrestrained, pagan delight, symbolized by the primroses, the whistling rustics, hooting owls, bleating sheep, grunting swine, and twittering birds (including the cuckoo), that surrounds and finally invades the Englishmen's false idyll.[60]

As indictments of alleged Arcadian virtues, *John Bull's Other Island* and *Purple Dust* reveal Shaw and O'Casey as two Irishmen excited by change and scientific progress. Certainly *John Bull's Other Island* reflects Shaw's antipathy for the degrading, brutalizing aspects of unscientific farming and emphasizes his persistent view of history as advancement from ignorance, superstition, and as obedience to love, freedom, cooperation, and creativeness. *Purple Dust* likewise embodies O'Casey's conviction that "A change invariably brings a profit, never a doom."[61] He adds:

> Millions of youngsters growing up today will never see a scythe in action, never hear the sharp, pleasant sound of hone-stone on a blade; never see the straining horses pull a plough,

> never see 'the ploughman homeward plod his weary way,' for all have gone and we have now the much more effective tractor and combine-harvester. . . . So Stoke and Poges . . . will inevitably be destroyed by those who are ready and eager to build better than the others knew.[62]

Despite O'Casey's acknowledgment of his fondness for Shaw's play, and despite the numerous similarities between the two works, O'Casey denied—in a vigorous letter to this writer—that *Purple Dust* was imitative of Shaw's drama:

> No. What put that into your head? Neither of the two Englishmen represented in *Purple Dust* is in any way similar to Broadbent, unless the bond of humanity unites a clever man with two damned fools. These two fellas do not typify the pride and sentimentality of the English; for the English are a courageous and intelligent people, with an old fool among them here and there, and two of these fools appear in *Purple Dust*. That is all.

So O'Casey phases out the middle period of his dramatic development by recording the disappearance of a decayed and disintegrating verisimilitude and by delighting in the emergence of an O'Killigain vision, a vision that, while not oblivious of Ireland's heroic past, is oriented toward a brave new world, a vital, pragmatic present, embracing both love and labor, passion and productivity.

FOUR

ARISTOPHANIC ALLEGORIES: MYTH AND MAGIC

> It isn't the clergy alone who booh and bluster against this joy of life in living, in dance, song, and story . . . who interfere in the free flow of thought from man to man. Playwrights and poets have had, are having, a share in squeezing the mind of man into visions of woe and great lamentations. . . . Political fellas in the U.S.A., in the U.S.S.R., in England, and especially in Ireland—everywhere in fact—political fellas run out and shout down any new effort made to give a more modern slant or a newer sign to any kind of artistic thought or imagination; menacing any unfamiliar thing appearing in picture, song, poem or play. They are fools, but they are menacing fools, and should be fought everywhere they shake a fist, be they priest, peasant, prime minister, or proletarian.—O'Casey's "Lively Credo"

O'Casey delineates and denigrates two puritanical, proselyting priests who boo and bluster against the joy of life and their small regiments of obedient followers—bourgeois bigots, religious radicals, and lewd-minded lackeys—in *Cock-a-Doodle Dandy* (1949) and *The Drums of Father Ned* (1960), two Aristophanic allegories designed to diagnose Ireland's major malignancy as excessive and repressive clerical authoritarianism—a clerical control that breeds a pathological obsession with the pleasures of the flesh and a cultural stagnation.

The caped and cruel crusader, Father Domineer, and his followers are victorious in the first play, shouting down imaginative but dangerous writers, chasing vital and hopeful people out of the village, and instilling visions of woe and worship in the minds of those who remain behind in the depopulated, desolate village. Yet the reverse is true in the second play, in which Father Fillifogue and his middle-aged supporters are dazed and defeated by an enlightened and resourceful legion of young people. The latter are inspired by Father Ned, a priest who symbolizes (like the cock in the earlier play) the prime mover, the invisible agent of conviviality and creativeness that gives rise to the Tostal, a national festival embracing many aspects of international life. Indeed, the young people are, like Ayamon Breydon in *The Star Turns Red*, committed to a liberated Ireland free of censorship, clerical tyranny, and economic and political bondage; and their program for future action synthesizes the heroic idealism of Ireland's past, Gaelic myth and legend, with certain aspects of Christian socialism. They dream, to be sure, of a brave new Ireland.

It is not, however, this focus on Ireland's future or on Ireland's problems with some of her priests that explains the extraordinary appeal of these plays for many students of drama. Rather, it is the montage of methods—the dazzling display of dramatic strategies and styles—that imparts to these extravagant fantasies their unique charm, vividness, and verve. Indeed, O'Casey is a virtuoso seemingly bent on experimenting with—juxtaposing and joining—all the paraphernalia and patterns in his large arsenal of theatrical techniques and tableaux in these late plays, which are distinguished, as are many of the poetic, modified Nō plays of William Butler Yeats, by a conscious and clever commingling of the mundane and the mysterious, the feasible and the fantastic. Ritualistic processions, music and dance, special lighting, offstage sounds, flashbacks, dream sequences, sudden disappearances, strange metamorphoses of people, birds, and objects, recurring symbols, choral voices, and emblematic or symbolic figures (all moving against evocative, colorful, and constantly changing landscapes) combine to give these plays a range and a resonance—a medley of moods and mannerisms—not to be found in any of the earlier works. Indeed, the verisimilitude and vision are, at intervals, almost indistinguishable in these comic-sad chiaroscuros.

COCK-A-DOODLE DANDY: CLERICAL BLACKNESS IN THE GREEN GARDEN

> Obviously there are few stories with such a universal appeal in the western world as that of the just man, unjustly persecuted and done to death, who by his brave dying creates faith. . . . But it must not be forgotten that underlying this tragic action, which to Christian belief is the Divine Comedy of salvation, can be found the remains of the much older cults, the Orphic, the Dionysiac Mysteries of the Greeks, the Hebrew ritual of the Day of Atonement, the Egyptian rite of Osiris. All these cults, centering on sacrifice and the ensuing purgation, seem to provide ever significant symbols for the expression of human guilt and its riddance.—Winifred Smith, "The Dying God in the Modern Theatre"

It is not the increasingly melancholy mood or the magic so much as it is the myth—the manipulation and modification of myth—that is to concern us in *Cock-a-Doodle Dandy*. Because of the many significant discoveries made by contemporary anthropologists and psychologists—Sir James Frazer's investigations of fertility worship among primitive, agricultural peoples and Carl Jung's theoretical notion about the "collective unconscious" in all men, to cite but two—modern writers have become increasingly fascinated with recurring patterns—archetypes—as they manifest themselves in myths and rituals of an immemorial nature. Consciously or unconsciously inspired by this complex heritage of ancient oral and literary forms, forms frequently reflecting a ceremonial conception of life, modern writers have deliberately attempted to devise their own imaginative equivalents for these primitive paradigms.[1] Yet often the work in the present does not duplicate exactly the primitive analogues; rather, the modern artist will manage and manipulate these fundamental, antique prototypes, modifying them to suit his rationally rehearsed objectives as spokesman—as poet-priest, perhaps—for his complex culture. Accepting and yet transcending the heritage of ritual and pageantry, the modern author attempts, therefore, to diagnose the dilemma of his own age while simultaneously relating his fiction to a much older tradition, thereby lending universality and depth to his writing.[2]

Specifically, the modern author often invites us to see his work as a reflection of his age and of all ages—as a work that both investigates particular personalities and problems in particular circumstances and yet relates to persistent and recurring patterns—to the larger rhythm of continuing life itself. In brief, the modern artist is apt to concede that, although the rhythm underlying the action is basically the same, the characters, costumes, and choreography are different.

Such appropriation and manipulation of ancient myth for satiric indictment is apparent in Sean O'Casey's dark comedy and fantasy, *Cock-a-Doodle Dandy* (1949), a drama that studies—indeed emphasizes—the antagonism between the Irishman and his milieu,[3] and that suggests that history is a recurrent, often depressing pageant consistently and rhythmically punctuated by acts of violence—the abuse, exile, or destruction of man, especially innocent, idealistic man. To emphasize the cruel continuity in human history—the sacrifice of innocents—O'Casey utilizes ancient scapegoat ceremonials as the formula for arranging and accenting his material, thereby charging his play with a symbolism that is encyclopedic and multidimensional.

The basic pattern in most scapegoat rituals, according to Frazer, involves a three-part movement. First, a sin-saturated community isolates one especially talented, handsome, or possessed individual as its leader or representative; the community subsequently pays extravagant homage to this hero-scapegoat for a brief interval of time; finally, the community exiles or kills its hero. The sins and guilt feelings of the community, concentrated in the victim-hero, are expiated by his departure or death, and so the community is free to live in relative peace and security until the cyclical pattern demands another crucifixion for community cleansing.[4] In his discussion of Shakespeare's Falstaff as a mock scapegoat-king, C. L. Barber likewise summarizes the scapegoat ritual—the process of purification by sacrifice—as one concerned with a sacrificial figure who sins for the sake of society, suffers for society in suffering for his sin, and ultimately carries his sin off into exile or death.[5]

The satiric extravaganza *Cock-a-Doodle Dandy* duplicates virtually all the main aspects of scapegoat ceremonies with some significant omissions and drastic alterations. Loreleen, an attractive, intelligent young woman with a jaunty air and a zest for life, is the scapegoat figure who, after an enlightening sojourn in London, enters Nyadnanave (nest of knaves), a puritanical Irish village obsessed with prayer, penance, and piety. The 1st Rough Fellow aptly describes the village as a place of "rough stones, th' twisty grass, an' th' moody misery of th' brown bog."[6] As defender-performer of the Dionysian dance, Loreleen puzzles and indeed frightens her conservative, conformist father, Michael Marthraun, who attempts to explain his daughter's dynamism by asserting that "she's either undher a spell, or she's a possessed person."[7] With her vitality, beauty, and provocative manner, Loreleen, like her namesake, the Lorelei of German legend, quickly attracts a flock of followers who have had quite enough of the incessant concern for sin and self-denial in the village. The 1st Rough Fellow, responding quickly to this lovely intruder, aptly describes her as a "Deirdre come to life again, not to sorrow, but to dance,"[8] and Sailor Mahan, owner of a fleet of lorries in the village, attempts to win Loreleen's affection by dancing with her and praising her "lovely face an' charmin' figure." Even the women of the house, Lorna, Marthraun's second young wife, and Marion, the house maid, are inspired to reject drudgery for dance and don gay raiments to participate in the singing and dancing.

However, with the arrival of Father Domineer, a cruel, arbitrary cleric who demands instant obedience from his parishioners and who denounces Loreleen as a "honied harlot" and "sinful slut," the villagers turn on Loreleen and stone her. Terrified and humiliated by Father Domineer and his cowardly followers—ironically, the two Rough Fellows are among the leaders in the manhandling of the young woman—Loreleen, her clothes torn and her face bloody, is finally dragged into Father Domineer's presence in the garden outside Marthraun's house. Determined to see that she inspires no more sin in the village's "virtuous bordhers," he sends her into exile: "Get away from here quicker than you came, or it's in your coffin you'll be."[9]

With the departure of Loreleen, who is joined by the vital Lorna, Marion, and Robin Adair, the town relapses into the stagnation of religious bondage it had previously known. Father Domineer summarizes the situation when he tells Michael: "th' demon is conquered—you can live peaceful an' happy in your own home now."[10] The play ends as Michael, fingering his rosary beads in a mood of despair, candidly observes: "I've no one left to me but th' Son o' God."[11]

Loreleen: Exile Follows Exultation

In keeping with her role as scapegoat figure involved in the spiritual sickness and potential purgation of the village, Loreleen also assumes, in a muted, less obvious manner, the dimensions of a fertility figure whose personal fluctuations—

changes in physical-psychological conditions—are correlated with corresponding changes in the natural world. Indeed, the progressive stages in her career—dancing, despairing, and departing—are synchronized with the three scenes that record the mutations in nature. It is not surprising, therefore, to discover that Loreleen is frequently associated with the color green—she wears a darkish green dress and bright green hat when she enters in Scene I—and with tall palms and scarlet flowers.

Called a "flower" by the 2nd Rough Fellow, Loreleen also wears a scarlet ornament on her hat, an ornament suggestive of a cock's crimson crest, and it is the dancing cock, with his agile movements and vivid colors, who is consistently identified with the life force that ripples through both man and nature in the play.

Scene I, when Loreleen, appearing as a dancing devotee of Dionysus in a puritan wilderness, is confident and hopeful, takes place on a brilliant summer morning as sunflowers, buttercups, and daisies bloom in the green garden, which, because of the long, oppressive heat wave, is beginning to take on a deep yellow hue. Scene II—Loreleen is now encountering fierce opposition from Father Domineer who talks of shipping her off to America—takes place at noon of the same day. As Loreleen is less hopeful, so too "the sunshine isn't quite so bright and determined." Scene III—Loreleen has now come to realize that she can't liberate the villagers from their condition of gloom and religious bondage—occurs appropriately at dusk of the same day, a day now much colder. As Loreleen has been suffocated by clerical blackness, so too have the vivid reds, greens, and yellows been replaced by sombre colors. The sun is setting, the sunflowers are a solemn black, and the house and flagpole in the garden have a dark aspect.

Thus O'Casey has apparently fused certain prominent features of scapegoat-fertility rituals in the career of his vital young woman who attempted to bring life to the village and to their green garden, an Irish microcosm. The glorious rebirth of life in the subsequent morning is not, however, going to occur. The villagers, surrounded by dead flowers and withering grass, will remain in the dusky evening of discontent. Father Domineer, representing a death-in-life that denies the libidinal energies of man, remains to dominate their lives as they "embalm" themselves with money and wait for death. The action in *Cock-a-Doodle Dandy* is, therefore, clearly arranged as a ritual, yet a ritual aborted. As Northrop Frye has asserted, the ritual pattern behind the catharsis of comedy depends heavily upon the return or resurrection that follows the departure or death of the hero, a resolution that often contains hints of the ancient ritual pattern of the victory of summer over winter, the green world over the grey.[12] However, O'Casey presents us in this play with an ironic foreshortening of the death-resurrection pattern. Deliberately discarding the motifs of redemption and resurrection central to scapegoat-fertility procedures, he emphasizes the despair, departure, and death that inevitably occur when an island of people fences itself off—a stone wall, four-feet high, surrounds Marthraun's garden—from the rest of life.

So O'Casey modifies the myth to accentuate the trauma and tyranny of a sin-sick society intent on preserving its old, confining traditions, especially the religious ones. Tragically, the black world defeats the green one.

Ritual Regulates the Action

Careful examination of the play's internal evidence justifies this reading. Scene I delineates Nyadnanave as a place of avarice, terror, hypocrisy, and a brooding, compulsive concern with sin. The 1st Rough Fellow captures the mood of the community when he declares that "young men should think of good-lookin' things in skirts only in the' presence of, an' undher th' guidance of, old and pious people."[13] Michael, bog-owner, village councillor, justice of the peace, and "fair-haired boy" of the clergy, defends the status quo and denounces "materialism" as a revolt against Christian conduct; he is especially dismayed because his lovely wife has taken to wearing "dismayin' decorations." And old Shannar, a superstitious, self-appointed soothsayer, likewise laments the "scourge of materialism" that is sweeping the world, citing the "circumnambulatory nature of a woman's form" as the chief source of difficulty.[14] Thus the village is depicted as a tradition-manacled Irish Eden, a green garden of ignorance and deceit where the men must conceal their lustful moods behind sanctimonious masks. Recoiling from women as evil creatures bent on man's damnation, the men of the village must behave like virtuous champions of the church fascinated with "th' four last things—hell, heaven, death, an' th' judgment."[15]

Into this heart of darkness and priestly paralysis comes Loreleen, who promptly lectures her father and his companion Sailor Mahan on the folly of laying up treasures on this earth. Declaring that she is "seeking happiness," Loreleen exerts herself to liberate the women from conditions of domestic slavery, bringing them forth into the light of the living. Affirming that the women must bring a "spray of light" into the dark village by laughing, dancing, and loving, Loreleen defiantly lectures Father Domineer on his myopic, Jansenistic view of woman: "When you condemn a fair face, you sneer at God's good handiwork. You are layin' your curse, sir, not upon a sin, but on a joy."[16] Citing the latent lust that inflames the men when a "skirt passes," Loreleen speculates that if God had given tusks to the village males, they would "rend asundher every woman of th' district'."[17] Predicting her own later departure, Loreleen despairingly cries out: "Is it any wonder that th' girls are fleein' in their tens of thousands from this bewildhered land?"[18]

Loreleen's savage indignation and courageous optimism are,

however, no match for the gloomy traditionalism of the adamant Father Domineer, who is supported by a number of unthinking, unmerciful disciples like the Bellman, the Sergeant, and One-Eyed Larry, whose physical defect defines his mental limitations. Responding in lock-step fashion, the villagers flock to Domineer's standard, and he marshals them into formation like a priest-general of the church preparing for a holy crusade:

> Stop where yous are! . . . No hidin' from the enemy! . . . Shoulder to shoulder, an' step together against th' onward rush of paganism! Boldly tread, firm each foot, erect each head![19]

Savagely condemning Loreleen and her supporters—Robin Adair, the cock, and the women—for destroying the desire for prayer and obedience in the district, Father Domineer dispatches Loreleen from the village, demanding that she "crawl in th' dust, as did th' snake in th' Garden of Eden."[20]

Visibly shaken, harrowed by the hell in Nyadnanave, Loreleen departs, joined by Lorna who exclaims: "Lift up your heart lass: we go not towards an evil, but leave an evil behind us!"[21] The community has not been purged of its melancholy mood or its sin-sickness; the catharsis could not occur. So the sad villagers, bereft of the vital men and women, assume stooped, sagging postures beneath the canopy of the darkening summer sky. In place of the warmth of wine and women, they are left to finger their rosary beads, which are obviously symbolic of the clerical chains that bind them fast.

Nyadnanave as Microcosm

Emphasizing the theme of exile that is so common in modern Irish literature, *Cock-a-Doodle Dandy* synthesizes ancient ceremonial formulas to censure severe, inflexible custodians of conduct too quick to punish free spirits who enjoy "bad books, bad plays, bad pictures, and bad thoughts!"[22] Moreover, O'Casey obviously sees the tragedy of Nyadnanave as part of the larger, recurring scheme of intimidation, terror, and exile so common to all cultures:

> Father Domineer is the symbol of repression. The incidents in the play, killing of a man, maltreatment of the young woman, actually happened in Ireland (and many more) but he also symbolizes all things which suppress life: conditions under which we live as well as domineering personalities of priests, potentates, or politicians—Joe McCarthy.[23]

Later, in a long and informative letter, O'Casey, while endeavoring unsuccessfully to recapture the mood he was in when he wrote the play, identifies two songs that influenced the drama's composition; he comments upon the historical and symbolic significance of the cock, and then concludes by emphasizing the larger implications of the work, a work not restricted solely to "walled-in" minds in Ireland:

> It is impossible after such a long time, to really explain the ideas and emotions that went into the making of COCKADOODLE DANDY. Here are some answers however:
>
> 1. The name was given to me by the well-known song ROBIN ADAIR.
>
> 2. Oh, I thought it plain by the context of the play that the COCK meant life, energy, alertness, courage. This fowl is a world symbol, familiar to Shakespeare. It is a symbol for France. It is the "bird of dawn"; the "hearld of the morn", and, according to Shakespeare, when Christmas came, it "sang all the night through". At one time it was believed that an effigy of this bird protected a home or building from evil—hence the weather-cock or weather-vane.
>
> 3. Yes, in many ways, but more expressive of repression, of banning, and, generally, of all efforts everywhere to prevent differing opinions being held and exclaimed when they happen to go against tradition, custom, belief, of self-interests—com-

mon occurrence in most places, not alone in poor Ireland. You have this habit even in your own country—the Real McCoy or the Real McCarthy.

4. You can think this way, if you like; but walled-in spaces are everywhere; walled-in beliefs, smiting any head which tries to pass through or by them. Some time ago, a Pope's Domestic Prelate, Monsignor O'Duddy, head of a High School in a Southern State, told children's parents that no pupil would be allowed to dress in jeans and jersey, because such things tended to make Communists of them! A walled-in mind. By the way, the play's title was suggested by George Cohan's Yankee Doodle Dandy!

In another letter O'Casey refers to the "twisted visions" in Michael Marthraun's mind and hints that Marthraun's response to reality is symptomatic of the pervasive superstition in Ireland, superstition that often makes progress difficult. He also alludes to the Irishman's fearful attitudes toward sex, the cause of the tragedy of alienation in *Cock-a-Doodle Dandy:*

Your last questions are just impossible to answer for it isnt possible for me to go back to the mood in which I wrote COCK-ADOODLE DANDY. Few authors can do it. I daresay that the twisted architecture of the house and porch are indicative of the twisted visions in Marthraun's mind. A twisted mind that saw demons everywhere, horns on the heads of the women, demon in bottle of whiskey, etc.

These things were common in Ire. and still are. Few weeks ago work on a new road was stopped because it necessitated the cutting away of thorn trees. The Peasants would not allow it, and eventually the road had to go around them. Stories of one-eyed larries who had eyes pushed out by a demon thumb are told round the firesides. The scene and story of Lorelei in the play is a fact and appeared in the public Press; and it is well known that sex in Ire. is abhorrent. Last week, a Limerick priest got ten thousand members of a confraternity, the women of Legion of Mary, the Civic Guard (Ire.'s police) to undertake the driving from the cinemas the young couples who cuddled together while watching a picture; it is the talk of Dublin, but there is no public protest at this violent suppression of the irresistible urging of sex in adolescence. The killing of the man in the play actually happened a few years ago, for the reason given, he refused to give up living with a woman. The violent scene in BEHIND GREEN CURTAINS actually happened, and a young girl was tied to a telegraph pole in her night dress, and left there through a frosty night, till the postman found her half dead next morning. Now, I can answer no more ques. O I am nearly blind and the work is imposs. I have to guess at this typing

THE DRUMS OF FATHER NED: THE IRISH HAVE GONE TO THE FAIR

O'Casey returns to another Irish village, Doonavale, in *The Drums of Father Ned*, for he had discovered, as he confesses, that "(like Joyce, it is only through an Irish scene that my imagination can weave a way), within the Irish shadows or out in the Irish sunshine, if it is to have a full, or, at least, a fair, chance to play."[24] Resentful of being the town of the "shut mouth" where fearful people refuse to reveal their basic emotions or express their real convictions—the town of coin collecting and book banishing—the young of the village demonstrate what could have happened at the Dublin International Festival of 1958 as they transform Doonavale into a green and pleasant place—a town responsive to Bach and Brian Boru, to flowers and fencing, and to dance, debate, and drama.

O'Casey applauds the courageous creativeness of the Doonavale youth in "O'Casey's Drama-Bonfire":

> The intelligent and educated Irish are, I believe, becoming impatient with, and resentful of, the interference of priest and bishop in every phase of their life. Some of them have spoken

> out, and even De Valera (Ireland's present Taoiseach—Prime Minister) has publicly repudiated the Bishop of Galway on a question of religious intolerance. I try to show this awakening, this thrust forward in thought, this new resolution, in my latest play, *The Drums of Father Ned.*[25]

Father Ned, the symbolic synthesis of the imaginative, courageous, and charitable aspects of some earlier Irish priests who had jeopardized their careers by fighting to bring more liberty and levity into some Irish villages of darkness and denial, is the catalyst behind the creative conduct of the young. Though he is never seen, we are made aware of his hovering presence by numerous references to him and by his intermittent drumming. An omnipresent figure with red hair, green eyes, and long white hands, Father Ned gradually increases in symbolic stature as the play progresses, and he slowly takes on the dimensions of a beneficent deity or Shavian godfather, an enlarged, never stationary, Ariel-like apparition in clerical garb who is surrounded by an aura of mystery and magical potency.[26]

While the parish priest Father Fillifogue, with his scorn for communism and for youthful desires and dress, and Fillifogue's adult supporters resent and fear Father Ned as a menace to both the community and the country, the youthful are quick to obey Ned's orders; they translate his advice into action, sprinting hither and yon to make flower boxes for window sills, to paint or adorn doors and lamp posts, to rehearse scenes, or to prepare posters and banners for the Tostal play and pageant. Anxious to preserve and promulgate the literature of Ireland's ancient past, aware of the libidinous drives in Ireland's young, and willing to struggle for a workable compromise between tradition and individual talent, Father Ned suggests that a solution to Ireland's future problems might lie in the fusion of the courage, comradeship, and heroic creeds of her rich past with the energy, enlightened social awareness, hopeful determination, and youthful optimism of her present.

Another symbolic figure who is continually alluded to is Angus the Young, who enhances the play's poetic dimensions and who figures in some of the discussions. Indeed, it is Angus who combines and concentrates much of the play's meaning in his person and paraphernalia. The Celtic god of youth and loveliness, he is associated with attributes that might constitute an O'Caseyan holy trinity: with his poetic face and long, black hair, he reminds us of youthful enthusiasm, the rapturous response to reality; with his harp, he becomes an Irish muse inspiring people to create in song, dance, and drama; finally, with his gaily plumaged bird, he is associated with flight, with nature's joyful sounds, and with soaring, singing aspiration. Moreover, the bird's four vivid colors give us a spectrum—a synthesis—of the drama's major concerns: the green of the breast points to the anticipated rebirth of life in Ireland in the Tostal spring festival; the black of his busy head reminds us of the always-arriving, always-looking Father Fillifogue (an obvious pun: the name suggests one who fills with fog—a befogger of minds and places) and his "Thou Shall Not" preachments; the crimson suggests an awareness of communism and of the timber-laden Soviet ship waiting to be unloaded at the Doonavale dock; and the gold reminds us, perhaps, of the excessive concern for coin, for profit, which motivates virtually all the actions of store owner Binnington, building contractor McGilligan, and visiting Ulster businessman Skerighan.

PRERUMBLE AS FLASHBACK

As previously indicated, the design of this festival play combines and changes some of the moods and mannerisms of the earlier works. Structurally, the drama has three acts and a Prerumble, the latter reminding us somewhat of the "prelude of the shadows" in *Oak Leaves and Lavender*. This Prerumble is a flashback to the 1920s, as some Black and Tans, sometimes resembling yellow and black statues, jibe and jeer at two of their prisoners, Binnington, the Freestater, and McGilligan, the Republican, against a background of flaming disorder. It is a vivid, eerie scene, slightly exaggerated, as vivid streams of red and yellow flames cause the street in Doonavale to be "outlined only in a dream-like way" and give "vague shapes" to the houses and shops. O'Casey indicates that the "scene looks like a sudden vision of an experience long past conjured up within the mind of one who has gone through it."[27] Like August Strindberg in *A Dream Play* (1901), O'Casey is here using a controlling consciousness (identity unknown) to shape and accent his materials. The slight distortion is like that associated with dreams, with painful memories. Moreover, O'Casey reminds us of the Strindberg of *The Ghost Sonata* (1907) in his use of time in this interlude. By merging past and present time in Strindbergian or Joycean fashion O'Casey causes the past to appear as if it were the immediate present, the here and now; he is, moreover, able to identify the factors in the past that make for continuing antagonism in the present, thereby demonstrating the continuity, the cause-and-effect relationship, in human affairs.

Two symbols tower over the strife-shaken landscape in this Prerumble. One is a dazzling white, tilted Celtic cross and the other is a silver church spire, two icons that introduce the conflict between Ireland's gay and passionate past—a pagan past of joyful self-indulgence—and a Christian present of daily self-denial, the idea which runs through much of the play. Indeed, the two factions in the fantasy eventually congregate around one or the other of these two rallying points: the old and ostensibly pious stand under the church spire as defenders of tradition and enemies of innovation; the young and enthusiastic respond to the Celtic cross, to Ireland's vigorous past, as the shield gilding episode in Act II demonstrates. O'Casey had used a similar scenic arrangement in *The Star Turns Red*, juxtaposing the outline of a church with a factory and its many chimneys.

We hear Echo, an offstage onlooker and appraiser, in this opening movement, and his interruptions sometimes momentarily stall the drama's advance, providing us with an "outside" point of view, a detached voice that repeats and reiterates so as to expose and undermine. This swift opening scene ends when the Black and Tans flee a Sinn Feiner ambush, permitting Binnington and McGilligan to escape as they crawl off stage in opposite directions. The Prerumble's ending is like its beginning, with villagers chanting offstage about the Tans' destruction of their town:

> The Black and Tans are blasting now
> Ireland's living into the dead;
>
> Her homes and shops in flames fall down
> In red ashes on her bonny head.[28]

Act I, occurring at high noon of an early spring day, exposes the smugness, commercial morality, and the satisfied complacency that permeate the town, which might be named Dimvale. Now thirty-four years older, Binnington, mayor and general store owner, is a status-conscious provincial who displays pictures of Michael Collins and St. Anthony of Padua in his home and attaches a gold cross and a silver harp to his mayoral chain to impress others with his patriotism and piety. Distressed by the Tostal preparations, Ireland's festival to recognize the cultures of the world, Binnington is too politic to oppose them, and he defines his basic credo to be one of "gettin' and holdin' " all you can while nodding to your neighbors and paying lip service to your religion. Distressed by the new "materialism," by the cost of his donations to the town's emerging choir, debating society, and drama club, and by the migration of Irish workers to England, Binnington applauds Father Fillifogue's strenuous efforts to defend the Pope's "social" teachings. He still despises but does business with McGilligan who, like himself, resents the efforts of the Tostal workers to enliven the town:

> BINNINGTON. Resucitatin' Ireland! It's a waste of time!
> MCGILLIGAN. An' a waste of money. You won't resucitate us by bringin' back shaddas o' men who done an' said things in a tormented time of long ago that have no bearin' on th' life we live today.[29]

Yet Nora disagrees with her father, insisting that the ideas of Ireland's old leaders are often as valid today as when first spoken, and Mr. Murray, Father Fillifogue's organist for the Church of Our Lady Help of Christians, agrees with Nora. Neglecting his duties at the church to rehearse the youthful choir that must sing the Tostal Song with "gusto," Mr. Murray aligns himself with the youthful rebels. Agreeing with Father Ned that the town must know more about the music of Bach, Schubert, and others, organist Murray delights in the chorus of the Tostal song which anticipates, not a grim, but a gay Ireland:

> Hurrah for th' Tostal O,
> That tempts us from sleeping O,
> When Erin sings and laughs and shouts,
> Instead of always weeping O![30]

The organist concludes the act by advising Father Fillifogue, who is appalled at the workers' alteration of his drab, modest town into a "grinning, gaudy whore," that Bach, Mozart, Angus, and others were appointed by God to bring joy and music to His people.

POSTER CONCEALS POPE

The conflict between the two factions, the conservative old and the creative young, is accented in the stage arrangements for Act II, set in McGilligan's drawingroom, which is virtually a duplicate of Binnington's. The part of the room being used by the young workers, an area strewn with flags, colored windowsill flower boxes, material for festoons, planks, and a number of pikes, resembles a "busy workshop," an area of cluttered creativeness. The part of the room reserved for the older generation creates a sharp contrast; it is filled with "stiff" furniture suggesting a formal, pompous, and "status quo" atmosphere. Moreover, the scenic design provides a strong hint that those committed to the religion of art will win out over those dedicated to the art of religion. A gaily colored, home-painted poster with announcements about the Tostal half conceals a picture of the Pope, reminding the villagers not of scheduled religious activities but of the impending festival events: hurling match, concert, opera, play, dance, and the fair itself. The slogan "We were DEAD and are ALIVE AGAIN!" is also visible.

This death-rebirth motif is picked up again in the act when Bernadette, maid to the Binningtons and McGilligans, assures Tom, the town carpenter, that "old fields" like Doonavale (presently a vale of doom) can still produce "new corn" as "wintry" minds are replaced by different minds concentrating on thoughts of "spring." Later, Bernadette hints that the spring Tostal celebration may result in May Day rites with young boys and girls lingering together for long and pleasant intervals of time. Continuing her references to fertility, she kisses her suitor, Tom, subsequently remarking that, as young lovers, they could have a glorious "garden" where virtually all the shrubs and flowers would be vigorous and free of blemishes.

Others in the town, however, have little time or inclination to reflect on flowers. Skerighan, the Ulster businessman anxious to conclude his business so that he may return to his home in the north, contributes to the mushrooming myth about Father Ned by telling the startled Father Fillifogue that he saw Father Ned standing naked in a lorry:

> SKERIGHAN. Not thot way, mon, for there wasna claithin' on a body that wasna there, but fierce green eyes shinin' lak umeralds on fire in a white face thot was careerin' aboot though stayin' stull as an evenin' star, starin' up tae me frum doon in th' valley below.[31]

As the young workers continue to swarm through the town to complete their preparations for the Tostal, hoisting their flag above the presbytery and responding to the rhythm of a pipe band, Mrs. McGilligan is inspired by the mood of the moment; she assembles a group of the townspeople into a circle around her Tostal flag, assuring all of them that the flag, with its lovely colors and symbols, properly represents all of Ireland's interests. Personal grievances are momentarily forgotten and the act ends as the many Catholics dance vigorously to Skerighan's "Protestant" song.

The opening moments of Act III focus on Mayor Binnington's son Tom and the Man of the Pike, a worker for the pageant who is gilding a shield that is to be adorned with the face of Angus the Young, his harp, and his bird of the four colors. Father Ned has advised the young men that others must know of the living legacy of the "old Irish gods an' heroes": Conn, Brian Boru, Columcille, the young Dumbo, and Cuchullain. Later, Nora indicates that Ireland must assert herself to let her present reflect the courage and conviviality so prominent in her past: "We're fightin' what is old and stale and vicious: the hate, the meanness their policies preach; and to make a way for th' young and thrusting."[32]

An extended and increasingly acrimonious religious debate

involving Ulsterman Skerighan and the townspeople follows as they attempt to isolate, define, and defend the different aspects of the Catholic and non-Catholic faiths and to guess at the essence of God. Quoting Stephen Dedalus (James Joyce) that God is a shout in the street, Michael adds:

> It might be a shout for freedom, like th' shout of men on Bunker Hill; shout of th' people for bread in th' streets, as in th' French Revolution; or for th' world's ownership by th' people, as in the Soviet Revolution; or it might just be a drunken man, unsteadily meandhering his way home, shouting out Verdi's . . . 'Oh, Le-on-or-a.'[33]

A series of revelations and strange occurrences enliven the play's resolution. First, Father Fillifogue discloses that Michael Binnington and Nora McGilligan will seek election as the town's two representatives to Erin's Dail; then, when organist Murray enters to announce that the people are flocking behind Father Ned's leadership to the town meeting on the Hill of the Three Shouts, Father Fillifogue declares that he will rally his forces, including the Town Clerk and Macekeeper; yet these drop dead as parts of "The Dead March of Saul" are heard. Then Binnington, McGilligan, and Father Fillifogue find themselves unable to "arise and go now," remaining in a "semistupified way" in their chairs. When Father Fillifogue asks "Oh, dear, what can the matter be?", the answer given is: "Ireland has gone to the fair!"[34] The antithesis of the Fili, bardic celebrants of vigorous life in ancient Ireland, Fillifogue resorts to clerical filibustering, dilatory tactics designed to impede the opposition's progress. With Bizet's March from "Suite, Maid of Perth" sounding in the background, the play ends as Echo identifies the distant roll of drums as that of Father Ned, a roll that, it is to be hoped, will set the people to dancing in both the North and South. A new Ireland pregnant with promise has emerged, and O'Casey, discounting the verisimilitude of businessmen and bigot, parades his vision, that of a playwright who longs for the rebirth of hope and hilarity in his native, green land.

As another gifted writer forming part of that incorrigibly Irish tradition of endless experimentation, O'Casey endeavors in his last phase to refine and reinforce his allegorical drama of multifarious tones and techniques. He obviously desires to elicit a new and illuminating intensity of awareness from his audience. Certainly these two late plays remind us that O'Casey's creative dynamics involve him in shaping—in making—a visionary art which will permit us to catch glimpses of the fluid frontiers of *his* visionary world. He would, like Eugene O'Neill, ask us to look *Beyond the Horizon*—taking us to the place where the contours of earth and sky meet. As a restless, poetic improviser, O'Casey strives to permeate his late dramas with the atmosphere of an ideal world, thereby imparting a lustre to a world bedimmed by custom. So he is, like Yeats and Joyce, both poet and priest, and his drama of multifarious radicalism approaches revelation, an incantation toward the good and the glorious.[35] It is truly a verisimilitude that both embraces and strains toward vision.

FIVE

O'CASEY CONFESSES AND COMMENTS: A LOOK AT HIS LETTERS

> Scalding dreams, thought Sean as he watched him dozing. The Irishman, most adaptable, least adaptable of men. Unique. So many of our greater ones living far from home, and dying there. So many. Darcy McGee, Canadian Member of Parliament, sinking down on the steps of a boardinghouse in Ottawa, with a bullet in his brain . . . George Moore in London, Shaw in Hertfordshire, Moore, the poet, in Wiltshire, Yeats in the south of France, Joyce in Zurich—not counting the innumerable flocks of Wild Geese. Oh, what strange fate brought you to such strange shrines?
> —O'Casey, "St. Pathrick's Day in the Morning"

My correspondence with Sean O'Casey began on February 18, 1959, when I was a graduate student at the University of Cincinnati, and ended on May 9, 1964, approximately four months before his death on September 18, 1964, of a heart attack in Torquay, England.

He sent me twenty-one letters, the majority of them written in response to questions I had asked him regarding subjects as diverse as his changing concepts of dramatic design; the complexities of his characters, major and minor; his literary relationships, notably with George Bernard Shaw and Eugene O'Neill; his recurring themes, leitmotifs, and symbols; his political and economic views; his quarrel with Irish Roman Catholicism, especially its myopic and repressive attitude toward sex; his respect for women (inspired primarily by his mother and his wife); his knowledge of and use of myth; the volatile and complex Irish temperament; the creative process; and the obvious biographical elements in his plays.

His letters, especially the early ones, which were written when he was relatively healthy and could still see well enough to type, are remarkable for their candor and completeness, for their levity and lyricism, and for their verisimilitude and vision. As his health deteriorated, the letters became noticeably shorter, staccato statements, reminding one of terse, elliptical telegrams. In some late instances, he quickly gave one sentence rejoinders to my queries; errors in spacing, punctuation, and spelling are understandably present in his final letters, and some words are difficult, if not impossible, to decipher. (Errors in spelling have been corrected, and the obvious abbreviations written out in my typed copies.) Yet he was always extraordinarily concerned and courteous in even the last letters; he ignored his own physical discomfort and failing eyesight (his wife Eileen read him the sonnets of Milton and Shakespeare in the final months)[1] to identify an influence, to supply new data, or to modify an interpretation.

And with his final letter, when he apologetically gave me to understand that he could neither write any more letters nor grant me an interview, I was reluctantly and painfully forced to recognize the fact that O'Casey, magnanimous man and weary Irish warrior, knew that death was imminent:

> Sorry. It will not be possible for me to see you when you come to England.

> I have too much to do, too many to see, and little time in which to do the things or see the visitors. I have written you many times, and answered innumerable questions, and am too old and tired to do more. My time and energy are committed from now on till the coffin comes. Sorry about this, but blame the years that press down upon me.

What follows are some illuminating and at times amusing excerpts from these letters, pregnant passages which reveal O'Casey's abiding social consciousness, his extensive reading in American literature, and his relationships with men like Padraic Pearse and Jim Larkin; also revealed are his distrust, indeed hatred, of authoritarian inquisitions like those conducted by the late American Senator Joseph McCarthy; his fascination with Irish folklore and with flags; and his obvious knowledge of Shakespearian drama, to cite but a few.

In his first letter of February 18, 1959, he admits of a special fondness for his one-act fantasy *Time To Go*, applauds my grouping of his plays into three categories, and then manifests a genuine humility and a vigorous social awareness:

> Thanks for your letter—and it is some letter! You must be a busy man what with your work towards graduation, your work as a teacher of drama, your work as a husband and a father; enough, God knows, for any man to do.
>
> Yours is a very clever letter, and it answers itself the questions that you ask of me. Indeed, answers more than I could do, even if I should spend a week thinking them out.
>
> You know more about my "structural skill, vitality" and the rest, than I do; well, maybe, not more about the vitality, for that is a possession of mine own; so I can say no more about these than you have probably said, or may say, in the work you are doing. One query, however: Dont you think you might have chosen a better playwright than I to spend time and thought on? I am always worried a little when I learn that teacher or student are delving into work of mine to see what they can make of it, what they can lift up out of it. What about your own great O'Neill?

Your first (1) contention is, I think, mainly correct; but the sense of form within me isnt altogether conscious; not always deliberate, but, at times, instinctive; but in the main you are right. Your 3rd (3) point is correct, too. I am deeply committed to the work and thought of "raising the standard of living" in individual man and group; not materially alone, but in every manner and way that is grand and joyful, including the dignity of grief; but how this is to be done; or, rather the best way to do it, is the problem, and I hold that every living soul should be interested in solving it in one way or another. I like your division of the plays into the three catagories, though I am unable to say whether you are right or not. By the way, there's a bigger proletariat in the world than many think: you, for instance, are as much a proletariat as I am. All teachers are, however respectable they think themselves to be. All doctors, artists, clerks, customs officers; few of these are men of any property other than what they have for personal needs.

And, by the way, again, I'd like you to include the one-act TIME TO GO among the 'fantasies', for it is a play I like well. The picture you have is an old one. Under another cover by ordinary mail—I cant spend too much in air mail—I will send you one that is more recent. Now, goodbye for the present, with a farewell salute of warm regards to Mrs Rollins, to Sean, and to you. I like your epilogue that describes me as an ironic realist & dreamy Celt.

Two Knaves and a Queen

The letters that follow focus on aspects of his Dublin trilogy, *The Shadow of a Gunman*, *Juno and the Paycock*, and *The Plough and the Stars*, tragicomedies which mirror the alienation and anarchy that prevailed in Ireland during the time of the "Troubles," 1916–1923. Although O'Casey is obviously concerned with recording the tragically devastating impact of slum existence and nationalistic frenzy upon individual aspirations in these three early plays, he is likewise anxious to isolate and denigrate a major defect in his countrymen's character: their irrationality, their self-defeating romanticism, which causes them to be deceived repeatedly by meretricious trappings, by a flamboyant but false show. Indeed, his letters consistently assert that it was the Irishman's vanity—his fondness for histrionics and heroic masquerade—that made for so much of the confusion and chaos in Irish national life. He cites Donal Davoren, the dream-addicted poet, as a histrionic hero in this evaluation of *The Shadow of a Gunman* in a long paragraph from his letter of March 30, 1959:

> Question (1). Yes; we often chase after the wrong heroes, or those who are not heroes at all. There are countless heroes in the world, but few have ribbons in their coats, which is praise to God, for he doesn't care a damn about ornaments; though He stops to look at a great building or a fine picture; stays to listen to lovely music; pats a head that discovers something which gives man greater power and security, or gives to man the chance of a healthier life. This chasing of the hero is in the play; and also the readiness of poor conceited minds to be chased and honored for a heroism which is often foolish; though, of course, it remains true to believe that it is good to die for one's country (people, really) should the need arise. Old Glory is often fluttered for unworthy purposes, but the flag remains a true and beautiful symbol, even when held aloft by the hands of a scoundrel. We have to pay for vain conceits; and Davoren had to pay for his.

"Captain" Jack Boyle, the boastful boozer and morally bankrupt "paycock," is another histrionic hero in *Juno and the Paycock*, a masterfully modulated tragedy of vanity involving a Dublin tenement family of four shattered by a mixture of inertia and improvidence.[2] After revealing that Boyle was a "composite" of two characters, O'Casey then condemns the swaggering ex-sailor's self-indulgence in this passage from a brief letter:

> What a Questioner you are! "Juno": yes, of course, it is based on events in my life. All my plays, almost all, are based

> on events in my life; tho' Capt. Boyle is a composite of two characters.
>
> In a previous letter, you asked a question I forgot to answer. It was, Are you a Communist? Answer: Yes. Have always been a Communist; born one. thought the whole world knew it by now. Afterthought: *Juno* is a tragedy of vanity and of relinquishment to vanity. There are many Captain Boyles in this world—in love with their own images. Most of us have minor vanities but they do not cripple our ability to act sensibly. But the Captain and his parasitic companion have let their egos ruin their lives—and the lives of others. The Captain, intent on his personal glory, ignores his duties and disaster ensues; he is an Irish Narcissus.

Displaying righteous indignation in the face of "Captain" Jack's habitual irresponsibility is Juno, his wife and O'Casey's slum mother of sorrows, who struggles to protect and sustain her maimed son and discarded daughter. O'Casey's admiration for Juno, whose patience and compassion remind us of Joyce's Maria in "Clay," is evident in this paragraph from his March 30 letter:

> Question (2) You are right: Juno is a true hero, though unhonored and unsung; like thousands more, and this heroism is everlasting , for it is from God's heart and is the central pulse of Nature. I have known many such courageous women, young and old. The greatest saints have never been canonized.

O'Casey evokes the heroic world of classical mythology in this play, the title reminding us of stately Juno, sister and wife of Jupiter, Roman queen of heaven, and the protectress of women and marriage, who is sometimes associated with preening peacocks. Like her Roman counterpart, O'Casey's admirable woman struggles to salvage her marriage and protect her pregnant daughter, Mary. Yet "Captain" Jack, the Irish "paycock," refuses to attend—to protect—his Irish Juno, preferring to skip into Foley's pub in his faded plumage, soiled clothes, and a faded seaman's cap with its glazed peak. Hence we have a grotesque parody of the ancient classical arrangement, and O'Casey was aware that his title counterpointed the regal past and the fragmenting present, as his letter of December 4, 1960, reveals:

> Juno and Paycock–Yes, I have a recollection of the peacock's connection with Juno; and that the colored plumage of the great tail were the eyes of Argos, killed by Jupiter, I think, because he spied on him with his hundred eyes for Juno, who wanted to find out what Jupiter did and where he went—a fine connection with the play's title; and also, I liked the sound of it.

THE COVEY, ED SULLIVAN, AND JIM LARKIN

As was true of the two previous plays, O'Casey utilized people he had known and experiences he had shared in assembling *The Plough and the Stars*, that sophisticated symphony of the slums set during the abortive Easter Week rebellion of 1916.[3] O'Casey explains in the same letter of December 4:

> Covey. That was the name by which the lad, a smith's helper, who kept cold chisels, picks, etc., in order went. It is slang for a chap, a fellow 'Cove'; Covey had a 'derogatory' implication. Peter Flynn, on the same job, lighted fires, and made the tea, boiled the eggs, etc. for the workmen. I worked with them for about a year. The 'Young Covey' and Peter hated each other.

Incidentally, the Act II pub scene contrast between the swaggering drinkers and soldiers and the Orator, the contrast alluded to by O'Casey in his March 30 letter, reminds us of Joyce's use of a similar arrangement in "Ivy Day in the Committee Room," where the novelist uses Charles Stewart Parnell, the "uncrowned" king of Ireland, as a norm of excellence against which to measure the stout-sipping politicians and paudeens.

As we know, O'Casey's dramaturgy changes drastically in *The Silver Tassie*,[4] the antiwar play rejected by the Abbey Theatre directors. Yet O'Casey reiterates in his letter of March 24, 1960, his assertion that he never slavishly mimicked one work or adopted one dramatic mode, expressionism, for example, in this or his other middle and late plays:

> I never consciously adopted 'expressionism' which I don't understand and never did. To me there are no 'impressionistic', 'expressionistic', 'realistic' (social or otherwise) plays: there are very good plays and bad ones.

In a later letter, of February 26, 1962, O'Casey again refers to Robert Burns' Scottish ballad as the song responsible for initiating the creative chain of events behind his fourth major play:

> Question 1. 'Silver Tassie' has within it personal experience with the aftermath—going to the front and coming back—of those who took part in War No. I; but—see biography—was started off by hearing a friend singing Burns' song 'Gae bring tae me a pint o' wine.'

O'Casey's letter of March 24, the one praising Eugene O'Neill and *The Hairy Ape*, refers in a "derogatory" fashion to the Ed Sullivan television program. This critical reference is part of O'Casey's reaction to an unpleasant experience he had with the American impresario in 1960. Sullivan had invited O'Casey to be a participant on one of his shows but at the close of this program, which was designed to acquaint the large American audience with O'Casey's genius, Sullivan abruptly announced that O'Casey would not appear. Here is O'Casey's response to the cancellation:

> Ed Sullivan unintentionally did me a good turn by keeping me out of his stupid program. He invited by telegram Brooks Atkinson, Richard Watts, and Tom Curtiss—the drama critic in Paris for *Herald-Tribune*, and the poor lads accepted, sitting thro' an hour's horrifying triviality, to hear at the end that O'Casey had gone home. All three were damned angry, and no wonder.

O'Casey has little to say about *Within the Gates*, his Hyde Park play, except to mention that he did not regard it as a "Morality Play" (letter of July 25, 1959), but he has a cluster of comments to direct toward his two "Red" plays, *The Star Turns Red* and *Red Roses for Me*. He discusses the former, a polemical play making use of puppetlike people who shout manifestos,[5] in this brief passage from his letter of February 26:

> 'Star Turns Red' was, of course, a curse on the Nazi-Fascist powers; plus the attempt to form the 'Blue Shirts' in Ireland.

He objected vigorously, however, to my suggestion that the play embodied Communist Party ideology—Marxian dialectical materialism—in his letter of July 25:

> Star Turns Red: No: a victory for the workers which, of course, is part of the Marxian Dialectical struggle, but there is nothing of the Marxian Dialectical philosophy in the play. It is built, as G. B. Shaw saw, and declared in a letter to me, on the sentiments and protests and language of the Authorized Version of the Bible; plus the activity and outlook of Jim Larkin, the Irish labor leader, and things that happened then. It was as George Jean Nathan saw (see Preface to *Five Great Irish Plays*, Random House) a prophetical play. By the way, like Shaw, I was born a Communist, and have been one all my life. I was one long before I heard the name of Lenin, as was G.B.S.; and as a born Communist I am intensely interested in all phases of life, from the lilies of the field up to the stars in the sky.

AUTOBIOGRAPHY AND ALLEGORY

Red Roses for Me is, with some reservations, a portrait of the artist as Dublin poet and labor leader—of O'Casey himself [6] —as the two letters of December 4 and November 11, 1960, confirm:

> 1. All plays have something of myself in them; 'Red Roses', perhaps, more than most . . . Ayamonn in 'Red Roses' is semi-biographical, as is Dickens's 'David Copperfield.' There is something of me in most of my plays. If not actually biographical, I knew all the characters. In 'Drums of Father Ned,' for instance, Mr. Murray was parish organist I knew well—his name, even, isn't changed.

O'Casey's final letters focused on his satiric fantasies, his Aristophanic allegories: *Oak Leaves and Lavender*, *Cock-a-Doodle Dandy*, *Time To Go*, and *The Bishop's Bonfire*, the latter three excoriating materialism and the clerical authoritarianism in Ireland which nurtures a repressive, Jansenistic hostility toward the pleasures of the flesh. After agreeing with my interpretation that *Oak Leaves and Lavender*, an argumentative dance-debate-drama set in a manor house in Cornwall during the Battle of Britain, celebrated the tenacity and courage of the English and Irish in the face of a Nazi nightmare, O'Casey's class-consciousness surfaced and he lashed out at the leisured few who relax in manor houses while others toil for their comfort, in this long passage from a letter of October 2, 1959:

> Oak Leaves and Lavender. Right, on the whole. Life must become brutal in strife, otherwise it wouldn't be any damned good: one side would never get the other one down. 'Cry havoc! and let loose the dogs of war!'—not gentle dogs, mind you; not sent out to lick hands, but to bite throats; so we must do away with war and strife. However, the last wasn't a war for us—it was a fight for life, and it had to be waged; and, if we had lost it, whatever good there was in man—and there

> was a helluva lot—would have gone. As for 'gracious living'—this in a manor house here and a manor house there is *not* 'gracious living' but a selfish indulgence paid for in the sweat from other faces. To have a condition of gracious living, the whole nation must share it—all the people, all the time.

The one-act parable *Time To Go* (1951) resembles *Cock-a-Doodle Dandy* in its surprising intermingling of the natural and the supernatural, and O'Casey refers to this sprightly fantasy, revolving around Widow Machree and Kelly, as a parable on Mammonism in Ireland, in his letter of November 11:

> 'Time to Go' is an old Irish folk tale, just simply recounting how a woman weeping on a mossy bank, and asked, why, said she had sold a cow but had asked too much; and the man searching anxiously for the woman, because he thought he had given her too little for it: a parable, not about "honesty," but about warm-hearted generosity and thought for others. I have composed an elaborate background to the story, just as I did in 'End of the Beginning,' a world-wide folk-tale. Ireland is by and large in love, not with Jesus, but with Mammon. 'He made money,' said of a dead one, is the highest of actual monuments.

The Bishop's Bonfire continues O'Casey's assault on inflexible father figures, in this case Canon Burren and Councillor Reiligan, who refuse to encourage or help liberate the desires and dreams of the young people under their supervision, a severe policy that leads to discontent, neuroticism, and death. Set in Ballyoonagh, where "Thou Shall Not" is the cardinal commandment, the play exposes Ireland as a church-state, as O'Casey's letter of February 18, 1960, confirms:

> 1. Your thesis is generally a correct one, applying especially to Ireland. That is the apparent reality; but the symbolism is a wider one; it touches the state, the civil power, as well as the church; all organized institutions: Daughters of Freedom as well as the Legion of Mary; McCarthyism. Yesterday I had

two fine, eager, intelligent Russians here, prominent in Literary Russian Circles, and I found myself saying to one of them that 'he talked like a Catholic curate' (assistant priest). I noticed a USA postage appeal as a front on stamps asking anyone who 'received pornographic literature to report to Postmaster,' giving a golden chance to every fool of making a menace of life. We have to guard against all these—Prelate or Puricat.[7]

Dramatist O'Casey lauds the hopeful efforts of his young priest, Father Boheroe, Codger Sleehaun (who performs a choral function), and the idealistic Keelin, the liberal-minded contingent in this sad play with echoes of a polka, in his October 2, 1959, and February 18, 1960, letters:

Father Boheroe and 'The Codger' are partially alive, not fully so; none of us are, none of us can be—yet: we have a long way to go still. I'm sure the meeting between your kindly President and Mr. Khrushchev will speed us some distance on the way . . . [Boheroe] Not an *Ideal* priest (not enough fight in him), but a good man on the way to being better . . . There are a lot of Codgers in Ireland, with good heart and fine courage, but little education and no skill in using them. But I am one with the Codger and with Father Boheroe (the 'red Road') as far as they go; and Keelin too. However, your estimate is a fine one.

Finally, it seems appropriate to conclude with this extended sentence from his early letter of March 30: "Now, thank you for your kind words, though I venture to remind you of Whitman's appeal: 'I call to the world not to take the account of my friends, but to listen to my enemies, as I do.' "

Sean O'Casey

APPENDIX

R.G. Rollins, Esq. 18/2/59

Flat 3, 40 Trumlands Road, St. Marychurch, Torquay, Devon.
Tel.: Torquay 87766.

Dear Mr. Rollins, Thanks for your letter - and it is some letter ! You must be a busy man what with your work towards graduation, your work as a teacher of drama, your work as a husband and a father; enough, God knows, for any man to do.

Yours is a very clever letter, and it answers itself the questions that you ask of me. Indeed, answers more than I could do, even if I should spend a week thinking them out.

You know more about my "structural skill, vitality" and the rest, than I do; well, maybe, not more about the vitality, for that is a possession of mine own; so I can say no more about these than you have probably said, or may say, in the work you are doing. One query, however: Dont you think you might have chosen a better playwright than I to spend time and thought on ? I am always worried a little when I learn that teacher or student are delving into work of mine to see what they can make of it, what they can lift up out of it. What about your own great Ó Neill ?

Your first (1) contention is, I think, mainly corect; but the sense of form within me isnt altogether conscious; not always deliberate, but, at times, instinctive; but in the main you are right. Your 3rd (3) point is correct, too. I am deeply committed to the work and thought of "raising the standard of living" in individual man and group; not materially alone, but in every manner and way that is grand and joyful, including the dignity of grief; but how this is to be done; or, rather the best way to do it, is the problemn, and I hold that every living soul should be interested in solving it in one way or another. I like your division of the plays into the three catagoeies, though I am unable to say whether you are right or not. By the way, there's a bigger proletariat in the world than many think: you, for instance, are as much a proletariat as I am. All teachers are, however respectable they think themselves to be All doctors, artists, clerks, customs officers; few of these are men of any property other than what they have for personal needs.

And, by the way, again, I'd like you to include the one-act TIME TO GO among the 'fantasies', for it is a play I like well. The picture you have is an old one. Under another cover by ordinary mail - I cant spend too much in air mail - I will send you one that is more recent. Now, goodbye for the present, with a farewell salute of warm regards to Mrs Rollins, to Sean, and to you. I like your epilogue that describes me as an ironic realist & dreamy Celt.

Yours very sincerely: Sean O'Casey

Professor Ronald Rollins, 30/3/59.
University of Cincinnati.

Flat 3, 40 Trumlands Road, St. Marychurch, Torquay, Devon.
Tel.: Torquay 87766.

Dear friend,

Heaven helps us, for God makes us keep on trying; or he just lets us die. Glad you liked the Photograph, & I hope Mrs Rollins liked it, too; & tell Sean the old withered face once shone with youth like his own. As "the lad who got a letter & a photograph from O'Casey" won't get the lad any quicker into heaven — just you ask Cardinal Spellman.

Question (1). Yes; we often chase after the wrong heroes, or those who are not heroes at all. There are countless heroes in the world, but few have ribbons in their coats, which is praise to God, for He doesn't care a ~~[unclear]~~ about ornaments; though He stops to look at a great building or a fine picture; stays to listen to lovely music; pats a head that discovers something which gives man greater power & security, or gives to man the chance of a healthier life.

This chasing of a hero is in the play; and also the readiness of poor conceited minds to be chased and honored for a heroism which is often foolish; though, of course, it remains true to believe that it is good to die for one's country (people, really), should the need arise. Old Glory is often fluttered for unworthy purposes; but the flag remains a true and beautiful symbol, even when held aloft by the hands of a scoundrel. We have to pay for vain conceits; & Davoren had to pay for his.

Question (2) You are right: Juno is a true hero, though unhonored and unsung; like thousands more, & this heroism is everlasting, for it from God's heart of and is the central pulse of Nature. I have known many such courageous women, young and old. The greatest saints have never been canonized.

Quest (3) I think so, ~~though~~ there is many-sided vanities in the work: of the Covey, of Pete Flynn, of the brave Bessie, of the equally brave Fluther; of Clitheroe and his companion Captain. We have all some vanity or other; but mostly innocent ones; remaining innocent so long as we refuse to allow it to destroy or weaken our finer qualities. But the "Orator" is not vain; he is dangerous sincere; so sure that he is ready to kill or be killed for his Ideal, as many great men were — Washington, Lincoln, Kosciosko. I knew this 'Orator' well — Padraig Pearse, and there were none more charming, gentle, or brave than he; he was the only Gael I knew who defended Synge; he, & a buddy of mine Donal O Murchadha. You have drawn, I think, a fine & true face behind the Mask. A few minor mistakes: I started work at 14 — age allowed by law — not 13; as well as being "intense, rhapsodic, and fanciful", I was, God help me, often foolish. However, in my opinion, a very excellent "halo"; an earthly one, with, maybe, a ray from heaven in its earthiness — I hope so.

Now, thank you for your kind words, though I venture to remind you of Whitman's ~~[illegible]~~ appeal: "I call to the world not to take the accounts of my friends, but to listen to my enemies, as I do."

My many good wishes & warm regards to Mrs Rollins, to Sean, and to you.

Yours very sincerely
Sean O'Casey

July 25, 1959

Flat 3, 40 Trumlands Road, St. Marychurch, Torquay, Devon.
Tel.: Torquay 87766.

Dear Ronald.

It is hard to answer your question, for I'm not a critic. It may be that there is a lyrical rhythm in the plays — as you say — but there's also and always a lyrical rhythm, sad or comic, in Life; & the artist is forever trying to get this lyrical rhythm into his work — poem, picture, sculpture, or play; or, so I think. Whether I've managed to do this or not, I don't know. There is the same rhythm in our bodies — not always in our minds, unfortunately — and if this rhythm be interrupted, & a new rhythm introduced by bacteria or virus, we are downed, till the rhythm of life conquers, or the other succeeds over life, & then we pass into the still & silent rhythm of death.

Your first question (1): I wasn't "triggered off" in any particular way, or by any particular influence; that is, in playwrighting. For better or worse, I am a blend of experience & absorption of the spirit in the old, odd melodramas, which you never saw; of Shakespeare, & the Elizabethans; of Goldsmith, Sheridan, Shaw; with the insistent influence of the romantic poets; & of everything I read, including the Americans: Whitman, Jefferson, Emerson, Melville, Hawthorne, & Lincoln. In fact: a world of life is within me, and, I suppose, I have moulded it all into an O'Casey figure of color, line, & form in "The Silver Tassie" &

over

2

was done easily in 1st act, but the War Scene was a different problem. No one can put a war on the Stage, even Shakespeare or the Soviet playwrights. I wished to give the spirit of the war, & to show the Christian fighters that they slew & maimed each other before the face of the Son of God, tho' this idea was largely unconscious — it was there. I seemed to fall; so, you may say, I drifted into it, because there was no other way. So I turned from "realism"; though I'd written a one-act fantasy in 1924 — "Kathleen Listens In"; & it was not new to me.

3. W. the Gates. Probably could be, maybe is, a "Morality Play," tho' I didn't write it from that viewpoint.

Star Turns Red. No. A victory for the workers, which, of course, is part of the Mater. Dialectical struggle; but there is nothing of the M. D. Philosophy in the play. It is built, as G.B. Shaw saw, & declared in a letter to me, on the sentiments & protests & language of the Authorised Version of the Bible; plus the activities & outlook of Jim Larkin, the Irish Labor Leader, & things that happened then. It was, as Nathan saw (see Preface to Five Great Irish Plays, Random House) a prophetical play. By the way, like Shaw, I was born a Communist, & have been one all my life. I was one long before I heard the name of Lenin, as was G.B.S.; & as a born C. I am intensely interested in all phases of life, from the lilies of the field up to the Stars in the sky.

I hope you'll be able to make this writing out. ~~Eyes~~ Eyes not too good. Returned your money order; hope you got it. All the best to all.

Sean

Ronald H. Rollins, Esq. 2 Oct. 1959

Flat 3, 40 Trumlands Road, St. Marychurch, Torquay, Devon.
Tel.: Torquay 87766.

Dear Mr Rollins, I've been engaged with my eyes since your letter came — it is to be a struggle to read from this out, but I'm used to struggle. Your questions:

O. Leaves & Lavender: Right; on the whole. Life must become brutal in strife, otherwise it wouldn't be any damned good: one side would never get the other one down. "Cry havoc! & let loose the dogs of war!" — not gentle dogs, mind you; not sent out to lick hands, but to bite throats; so, we must do away with war & strife.

However, the last wasn't a war for us — it was a fight for life, & it had to be waged; &, if we had lost it, whatever good there was in man — and there was a helluva lot — would have gone.

As for "gracious living" — this in a manor here & a manor there is not "gracious living" but a selfish indulgence paid for in the sweat from other faces. To have a condition of gracious living, the whole nation must share it — all the people, all the time. "Cockadoodle Dandy": The Cock has been for thousands of years the symbol of rising, of virility, of courage, of outspokenness — its crow is clarion; the herald of the dawn. Father Domineer is the symbol of repression. The incidents in the play — killing of a man, maltreatment of the young woman, actually happened in Ireland (& many more); but he also symbolises all things which suppress life: conditions under which we live as well as domineering personalities of priest, potentate, or politician — Joe McCarthy! for instance. Professors & Teachers here with us and there with you, don't get the recognition of importance in dignity of status or measure of salary they need & deserve to allow them to develop & grow ~~they~~ the way they should & could if they are to give of their gracious best.

Father Boheroe and "The Codger" are partially alive, not fully so: none of us are, none of us can be — yet: we have a long way to go still. I'm sure the meeting between your kindly President & Mr Khruschev will speed us some distance on the way.

Eyes tired, so au revoir, a chara.

With Warm Regards to your wife and family and to yourself.

Sean

See other note--

18 Feb. 1960

Mr. Ronald G. Rollins.

Flat 3, 40 Trumlands Road, St. Marychurch, Torquay, Devon.
Tel.: Torquay 87766.

Dear Ronald: your questions —

1. Your thesis is generally a correct one, applying especially to Ireland: that is the apparent reality; but the Symbolism is a wider one: it touches the State, the Civil power, as well as the Church; all organized institutions: Daughters of Freedom as well as the Legion of Mary; McCarthyism. Yesterday I have two fine eager, & intelligent Russians here, prominent in Literary Russian Circles, & I found myself saying to one of them that "he talked like a Catholic 'Curate'" (assistant priest). I notice a USA Postage appeal as a frank on stamps asking anyone who "received pornographic literature to report to Postmaster", giving a golden chance to every fool of making a menace of life. We have to guard against all these — Prelate or Bureaucrat.

2. Not an Ideal priest (not enough fight in him), but a good man on the way to being better.

3. Not quite. All Kelts — bare the Mutes — sing. There are a lot of Codgers in Ireland, with good heart & fine courage, but little education & no skill in using them. But I am one with the Codger & with Father Boheroe ("the red Lord") as far as they go; and Keelin, too. However, your estimate is a fine one.

All the best to Mrs Rollins, Sean Og — & to you.

Sean O'Casey

(over)

Ronald Rollins, Esq. 24/3/1960
University of Cincinnati.
Cincinnati.

Flat 3, 40 Trumlands Road, St. Marychurch, Torquay, Devon.
Tel.: Torquay 87766.

Dear Rollins,

Ed Sullivan unintentially did me a good turn by keeping me out of his stupid program. He invited by telegram Brooks Atkinson, Richard Watts, and Tom Curtiss — Drama critic in Paris for Herald-Tribune, & the poor lads accepted, sitting thro' an hour's horrifying triviality, to hear at the end that O'Casey had gone home. All three are damned angry, & no wonder.

Your questions:

1. I wished to show the face & unveil the soul of war. I wanted a war play without noise; without the interruptions of gun fire, content to show its results, as in the chant of the wounded and the maiming of Harry; to show it in its main spiritual phases; its inner impulses and its actual horror of destroying the golden bodies of the young; & of the Church's damned approval in the sardonic hymn to the gun; as true today as it was then. I never consciously adopted "expressionism", which I don't understand & never did. To me there are no "expressionistic", "expressionistic" "realistic" (Social or otherwise) plays: there are only good plays and bad ones. Like your students, I think this play my best one; but the thought isn't important, & it may well be wrong.

2. I certainly would not say I was greater than the great O'Neill; not even as great as he; certainly not his equal in Philosophical thought. O'Neill is a giant of Drama — American and the world. I have a special affection for "The Hairy Ape", for it was praise of this play that gave me my first acquaintance with O'Neill. The great Irish Labor Leader, Jim Larkin, (of whom Bernard Shaw said "the greatest Irishman since Parnell") back from an Amer. visit, came to me in Liberty Hall, aglow with a play he had seen in N. York — "The Hairy Ape". "Get the play, Sean, when it comes — a great work. This fellow, O'Neill, will do things in the Theatre." And by God, he did, even in this early roaring rebellious Caliban striking out blindly, but getting nowhere, save at the end to be crushed to death by his choice of a brother: a symbol of the then Working-class, divorced from decency, from charm, from culture. Different now; but bad enough, with millions still in the state of the Hairy Ape, which explains the Ed Sullivan shows on television with you there, with us here; pandering to the ignorant & dull-brained boobs, worker & middle-class, bereft of any sense of music, art, or literature. O'Neill is like a great ~~oak~~ tree forever tussled about by a turbulent wind; & the "Hairy Ape" was O'Neill's loud shout on a first advent to the Drama.

3 Your students' guess is, I feel, a good one. As well, the Gaelic Language (which I know well) lingers through idioms in the English language as spoken by us; & this gives, at times, a curious lilt to Irish speech. By the way, we Gaels always pronounce "Celt" as "Kelt". The 'C' in Irish is always hard. Now a word to your students: Every man's first concern should be to himself. Don't bother too much about O'Casey. The world's beginning with you; ending with me.

To you, Ronald, my warm regards & to your wife & all of yours. Yours very sincerely

Osevor, Sean

Dr. Ronald G. Rollins.
Flat 3, 40 Trumlands Road, St. Marychurch, Torquay, Devon.
Tel.: Torquay 87766.

11 November 1960

Dear Ronald,

"Time to Go" is an Irish Folk Tale, just simply recounting how a woman weeping on a mossy bank, & asked, why, said she had sold a cow, but had asked too much; & the man searching anxiously for the woman, because he thought he had given her too little for it: a parable, not about "Honesty", but about warm-hearted generosity, & thought for others. I have composed an elaborate background to the story, just as I did in "End of the Beginning", a world-wide folk-tale. Ireland is by & large in love, not with Jesus, but with Mammon. "He made money", said of a dead one, is the highest of actual monuments.

Ayamonn in "Red Roses," is semi-biographical, as is Dicken's "David Copperfield." There is something of me in most of my plays, if not actually biographical, I knew all the characters. In "Drums of F. Ned", for instance, Mr. Murray was ~~xx~~ parish organist I knew well — his name, even, isn't changed.

"Cockadoodle Dandy": Yes, largely so, as you will see from a quotation given in "Figuro in the Night", when it appears in print next Spring. The latest book published in Gaelic is named "Saoirse gan so—" "Freedom without ease or comfort." The incident of the priest striking the worker is factual. The man was living with a woman; the priest struck, & the man died in a moment. Also the scene of attack on Loreleen is actual, & the priest's words are almost identical as those used by him. I have a Press account of it. Dances are (at times) squashed by Justices, advised by the local Bishops. Many people like "The Messenger"? Yes, many; but they have to remain dumb, & they have to stay still. Forgive terseness; I've had a tedious time with eye inflammation, & it is still troublesome. My love to Seamus — young John or Sean.

All good wishes to all.

As ever,

Sean aosta – Sean agus

Ronald G. Rollins, Esq. 4 Dec. 1960

Flat 3, 40 Trumlands Road, St. Marychurch, Torquay, Devon.
Tel.: Torquay 87766.

Dear Ron, I've been trussed up in bed with a virus infection, but am coming again, & fluttering about the room of life.

Your questions:

1 All plays have something of myself in them; "Red Roses", perhaps, more than most.

2. "The Bishop's Bonfire & the "Cock": there is a great deal of fact in both of them — that's why they are feared by certain groups.

The two incidents of the priest killing a man by a blow because he "lived in sin with a woman" is a fact; so is the scene of Lorelia beaten up by the crowd is a fact, with the priest's words almost verbatim. There are a lot of Seanaar's still in Ireland.

Your students are very generous — they have a far higher opinion of me than I have of myself.

Ballyoonagh has no special meaning. Nyadnanave — in Irish "The Nest of Saints", also, a play on words for Knave also has an implied meaning of a rogue — ~~[illegible]~~ ironical, of course

Juno & the Paycock — Yes, I had a recollection of the peacock's connection with Juno; & that the colored plumage of the great tail were the eyes of Argos, killed by Jupiter, I think, because he spied on him with his hundred eyes for Juno, who wanted to find out what J. did & where he went — a fine connection with the play's title; & also, I liked the sound of it.

Covey. That was the name by which the lad, a smith's helper, who kept cold chisels, picks, etc, in order. It is slang for a chap, a fellow: "Cove". Covey had a "derogatory" implication. Peter Flynn, on the same ~~job~~ job, lighted fires & made the tea, boiled eggs, etc for the workmen. I worked with them for about a year. The "Young Covey" & Peter hated each other.

I think that's all. Please give my love & warm wishes to your students.

as ever,

Sean

6 January, 1961

Flat 3, 40 Trumlands Road, St. Marychurch, Torquay, Devon.
Tel.: Torquay 87766.

Robert G. Rollins Esq.

Dear Robert,

What a Questioner you are!

"Juno": Yes, of course, it is based on events in my life. All my plays, almost all, are based on events in my life; tho' Capt. Boyle is a composite of 2 characters.

In a previous letter, you asked a question I forgot to answer. It was, Are you a Communist?

Answer: Yes. Have always been a Communist; born one. Thought the whole world knew it by now.

Warm regards

Sean

(See note)

Afterthought: Juno is a tragedy of vanity and of relinquishment to vanity. There are many Captain Boyles in this world--in love with their own images. Most of us have many minor vanities but they do not cripple our ability to act sensibly. But the Captain and his parasitic companion have let their egos ruin their lives--and the lives of others. The Captain, intent on his personal glory, ignores his duties and disaster ensues; he is an Irish Narcissus.

Flat 3, 40 Trumlands Road, St. Marychurch, Torquay, Devon.
Tel.: Torquay 87766.

15 April, 1961.

Ronald G. Rollins, Esq.

Dear Dr. Rollins,

I glanced at your venture into the spacious area of Ó Casey's promptings appearing in his plays; but I didnt try to read them for two reasons: first because I have to limit my reading (Eye-Doctor's orders); and, secondly because I never read, or rarely read, except when published, any opinions of thoughts that make comments upon what I have tried to do.

I get reams of these MSS asking me to comment, and were I to do so, my time would be up, my eyes gone, my heart broken.

My dear Ronald, I have more than Two faces ! I have many; but, by and large, I think you are right insofar that the two chief ones are realistic and lyrical (I hope).

Peter Balashov of the Gorki Academy of Science and the Arts, Moscow, in an article in a Soviet Magazine, says the same thing as you, comparing me to a well-known Soviet Asian poet; and a letter from Anne Elistratova, Union of Soviet Writers, who has just had a book published in the USSR on the Romantic Poets of England, that my biography reminds her of Byron's CHILDE HAROLD.

As for me, I do not try to influence anyone's comments about me (except on matters of fact), thinking that their opinions should go forth in their own way, and never in any way guided by me - maybe in the wrong direction.

I have contested critical opinions by -rish critics which I believed were set down in malice; but I am not going to interfere with serious and scholarly comments made in article or book about me; recognising that every man has a true morality, but that every man's true morality isnt the same -- Bernard Shaw.

The Young Lady, Warm Weather, hasnt come here yet, and only God knows when she will come. Fair health here, bar painful eye-inflammation troubling me, making things a bit more difficult½

My love to Sean, to Mrs Rollins, to you, and all.

Sean O'Casey

Flat 3, 40 Trumlands Road, St. Marychurch, Torquay, Devon.
Tel.: Torquay 87766.

15 Aug. 1961

Ronald Rollins, S.J.

Dear Ronald,

Couldn't reply before this. Eyes have been very bad, & still painful & troublesome. I am sorry to hear your Sean has been troubled in the same way; I hope the operation has been clearly successful, and that the ailment wasn't a serious one.

The above tells you, too, that I couldn't possibly read your MS. In fact, I am able to read or write but a little now: & every word written or read is a struggle under a powerful light.

That goes, too, for the Introduction. I am far behind with a lot which must be done; & go to London next week to see my Surgeon-oculist again, in the hope he might be able to make the vision (sight – is the English word) better by ½ per cent. A wan hope, I fear.

However, I'm 82, & Sean is young, but a gossoon; & his eyes are much more important than my old ones; so God be with them; strength, too, & clear sight: Amen.

Love to Mrs Rollins, & to you.

As ever,

Sean

September 17, 1961

Flat 3, 40 Trumlands Road, St. Marychurch, Torquay, Devon.
Tel.: Torquay 87766.

Mr. Ronald Rollins.

Dear Ron,

Yes, of course, you may use the quotation you mention. I dont mind the publication of anything I say or that I have said, provided that it is genuine - that my written name has been attached to it, and so nade certain that it was said or written by me. Many things have been printed as said by me, things never said; many of them extraordinarily stupid that I couldnt think of saying; and one cant be always writing to contradict these things; so I am responsible only for those sayings and opinions which carry my name at the end - which, I believe, is fair to all .

By the way, Robert Speight, the wellknown Eng. Actor (he was the creator of Becket in Eliot's MURDER IN THE CATHEDRAL), said of the TASSIe, in a letter defending it when it was violently denounced as blaspemous, etc, by the Irish clerics, that in this play O'Caey had snatched the veil from the hypocrisy and pretence of the Bourgeois, and had shown us al all the true horror and blasphemy of war; and that christian kil killed and maimed christian under the clear view of Jesus, the Son of Man.

He clearly saw the essence of the play.

It is still a struggle to read or write, but I fight on, though I've been stuck fast to the bed for the last fortnight with a bout of bronchitis, but expect to be better soon.

All the best ,
as ever,

Sean

P.S. You can print Speight's reference, if you wish.

Flat 3, 40 Trumlands Road, St. Marychurch, Torquay, Devon.
Tel.: Torquay 87766.

Aug. 14, 1962

Dear Ronald,

No. What put that into your head? Neither of the two Englishmen represented in *Purple Dust* is in any way similar to Broadbent, unless the bond of humanity unites a clever man with two damned fools. These two fellas do not typify the pride and sentimentality of the English; for the English are a courageous and intelligent people, with an odd fool among them here and there, and two of these fools appear in *Purple Dust*. That is all.

With all good wishes
As Ever
Sean

Dr. Ronald Rollins.
Marshall University,
Huntington,
W. Virginia.

Flat 3, 40 Trumlands Road, St. Marychurch, Torquay, Devon.
Tel.: Torquay 87766.

23/2/62

Dear Dr Ronalds

I was in bed from New Year's Day to the 19 Feb; stabbed thro' & thro' by Bronchitis plus plumbago, so couldn't even squint at your letters.

Question 1. "S. Tassie" has within it personal experience of the aftermath — going to the front & coming back — of those who took part in War no 1.; but — see biography — was started off by hearing a friend singing Burns's song "Go bring to me a pint o' wine." nothing else. "Within the Gates" nothing to do with Spain's war or any other war. "Star Turns Red" was, of course, a curse on the Nazi-Fascist powers; plus the attempt to form the "Blue Shirts" in Ireland.

2. Act 3. "Red Roses": Of course: a more safe, sensible, & colorful life for all Man. By the way, each of us is a unit in the Massmen. "Ayamonn" wants "that man might have life & have it more abundantly" — see New Testament.

Writing bad; no excuse to offer; hand a little shaky.

See also last issue of

over

"Modern Drama" magazine published by University of Kansas. Therein are a number of articles about my plays. symbolism, etc, including symbols in "Red Roses".

As ever.
Sean

Flat 3, 40 Trumlands Road, St. Marychurch, Torquay, Devon.
Tel.: Torquay 87766.

11 March, 1963

Ronald Rollins, Esq.,
Marshall University,
Huntington 1,
West Virginia.

Dear frien,

Your last questions are just impossible to answer for it isnt possible for me to go back to the mood in which I wrote COCKADOODLE DANDY. Few authors can do it. I daresay that the twisted archecture of the house and porch are indi cative of the twisted visions in Marthraun's mind. A twisted mind that saw demons everywhere, horns on the heads of the women demon in bott;e of whiskey, etc.

These things were common in Ire. and still are. Few weeks agom work on a new road was stopped because it necessitated the cutting away of thorn trees. The Peasants would not allow it, amd evenually the road had to go around them. Stories of one-eyed larries who had eyes pushed out bu a demon thumb are told round the firesides. The scene and story of Lorelie in the play is a fact and appeared in the public Press; and it is well known that sex in Ire. os abhorrent. Last week, a Limerisk priest got ten thoudand members of a confraternity, the women of Legion of Mary, the Civic Guard (Ire.'s police) to undertake the driving from the cinemas the young couples who cuddled together while watching a picture; it is the talk of Dublin, but there is no public protest at this violent suppression of the irreistible urging of sex in adolescence.. The killing of the man in the play actually happened a few years ago,for the reason given, he refused to give up living with a woman. The violent scene in BEHIND GREEN CURTAINS actually happened, and a young girl was tied to a telegraph pole in her night dress, and left there rhrough a frosty night, till the poastman found her half dead necxt morning. Now, I can answer no more ques. O I am nearly blind and the work is imposs. I have to guess at this typig

as ever,

Sean

To your students interested in Drama, I commend the Drama Criticisms & comments in the many books written by the late George Jean Nathan.

My eyesight is so bad now that I cannot read, and have to write & type by guesswork; so, if there are any mistakes in this letter, you will just have to [illegible]

Sean

Flat 3, 40 Trumlands Road, St. Marychurch, Torquay, Devon. England
Tel.: Torquay 87766.

Ronald Rollins Esq. 28 Oct. 1963.

ear Ronald,

It is impossible after such a long time, to illy explain the ideas and emotions that went into the making : COCKADOODLE DANDY. Here are some answers however:

1 The name was given to me by the well-known song ROBIN ADAIR.

2. Oh, I thought it plain by the context of the play that the COCK meant life, energy, alertness, courage. This fowl is a world symbol, familiar to Shakespeare. It is a symbol for France. It is the "bird of dawn"; the "herald of the morn", and, according to Shakespeare, when Christmas came, it "sang all the night through". At one time time it was believed that an effigy of this bird protected a home or building from evil - hence the weather-cock or weather-vane. .

3. Yes, in many ways but more expressive of repression, of banning, and, generally, of all efforts everywhere to prevent differing opinions being held and exclaimed, when they happent to go against tradition, custom, belief, of self-interests - common occurrence in most places, not alone in poor Ireland. You have this habit even in uoir own country - the Real McCoy or the Real McCarthy.

4. You can think this way, if you lke; but walled-in spaces are everywhere; walled-in belifs, smiying amy head which tries to pass through or by them. Some time ago, a Pope's Do,estic Pre;ate, Monsignor O'Duddy, head of a High School in a Southern State, told children's parents that no pupil would be allowed to dress in jeans and jersey, because such thins tended to make Communists of them ! A walled-in mind. By the way, the play's title was suggested by George Coham's Yankee Doodle Dandy !

My good wishes to all your Students and to you. Yours very sincerely,

Sean O'Casey.

Sean

over →

Flat 3, 40 Trumlands Road, St. Marychurch, Torquay, Devon.
Tel.: Torquay 87766.

Mr. R. Rollins. 9 May, 1964

Dear R. R.

Sorry. It will not be possible for me to see you when you come to England.

I have too much to do, too many to see, and little time in which to do the things (see the visitors. I have written you many times, and answered innumerable questions, and am too old and tired to do more. My time and energy are committed from now on till the coffin comes. Sorry about this, but blame the years that press down upon me.

Yours sincerely,

Sean O'Casey.

NOTES

Chapter One

1. *The Face and Mind of Ireland* (1950), p. 132.

2. *Three Great Irishmen: Shaw, Yeats, Joyce* (1957), pp. 22–23.

3. *Selected Plays of Bernard Shaw*, II (1949), pp. 446–47.

4. Ibid., p. 451.

5. Ibid., p. 448.

6. Ibid., p. 446.

7. Ibid., p. 517.

8. Ibid. Shaw points out that Doyle's special talents were "the freedom from illusion, the power of facing facts, the nervous industry, the sharpened wits, the sensitive pride of the imaginative man who has fought his way up through social persecution and poverty." Ibid., p. 445.

9. *Fiery Cross: The Story of Jim Larkin* (1963), p. 9.

10. W. I. Thompson, *The Imagination of an Insurrection: Dublin, Easter, 1916* (1967), pp. 82–85.

11. *Inishfallen, Fare Thee Well* (1956), p. 219.

12. See R. Ellmann, *Yeats: The Man and the Masks* (1958), p. 26.

13. *I Knock at the Door* (1956), pp. 148–53.

14. Ibid., pp. 242–56.

15. *Pictures in the Hallway* (1956), pp. 286–91.

16. *The Green Crow* (1956) p. x. In a letter of Feb. 18, 1959, O'Casey stated: "I like your epilogue that describes me as an ironic realist and dreamy Celt."

17. See *Sean O'Casey: Modern Judgements*, ed. Ronald Ayling (1970), pp. 166–76.

18. *Masters of English Literature*, 2, ed. Robert Pratt et al., (1963), pp. 824–25. See also *Yeats A Collection of Critical Essays*, ed. John Unterecker (1963), pp. 80–92, and my "Portraits of Four Irishmen as Artists: Verisimilitude and Vision," *Irish University Review*, 1 (1971), pp. 189–97.

19. *The Letters of W. B. Yeats*, ed. Allan Wade (1954), p. 63.

Chapter Two

1. Liam de Paor, *Divided Ulster* (1970), pp. 91–92.

2. Letter from O'Casey, July 19, 1963. See also R. Bennett, *The Black and Tans* (1963), pp. 18–20.

3. For a contrary view see D. Krause, *Sean O'Casey: The Man and his Plays* (1962), pp. 86–87.

4. *The Poet in the Theatre* (1946), pp. 8–9.

5. *Sean O'Casey: Modern Judgements*, pp. 23–24.

6. S. O'Casey, *Three Plays* (1960), p. 111.

7. Francis Fergusson's discussion of Chekhov's masterful use of ceremonial social occasions provided me with new insight into O'Casey's early dramaturgy. See *The Idea of a Theatre* (1949), pp. 174–79.

8. *Three Plays*, p. 130.

9. Ibid., p. 202.

10. Letter from O'Casey, Mar. 30, 1959.

11. *Three Plays*, p. 138.

12. "The Sources and Themes of The Plough and the Stars," *Modern Drama*, 4 (1961), p. 237.

13. Three Plays, p. 152.

14. Ibid., p. 140.

15. Ibid., p. 158.

16. *Drums Under the Windows* (1956), p. 241.

17. Letter from O'Casey, Mar. 30, 1959.

18. I am indebted to Joseph Frank's observations about the emergence of spatial form in modern fiction in this discussion of O'Casey's "polyphonic" technique. See *Criticism: the Foundations of Modern Literary Judgment*, ed. Mark Schorer, et al., (1958), pp. 381–85.

19. Hogan and S. E. Molin, *Drama: The Major Genres* (1962), p. 458.

20. *Three Plays*, p. 135.

21. Ibid., p. 144.

22. Ibid., p. 148.

23. "The Sources and Themes," p. 237.

24. *Three Plays*, p. 160.

25. Ibid., pp. 161–62. See O'Casey, *Blasts and Benedictions*, intro. Ronald Ayling (1967), pp. 97–98.

26. *Lady Gregory's Journals, 1916–30*, ed. Lennox Robinson (1946), p. 89.

27. *Three Plays*, p. 163.

28. Ibid., p. 177.

29. Ibid., p. 178. See also *The Imagination of an Insurrection*, pp. 210, 216–217.

30. "Sources and Themes," p. 240.

31. *Three Plays*, p. 178. See also R. J. Loftus, "The Poets of the Easter Rising," *Éire-Ireland*, 2 (1967), 111–21.

32. Ibid., p. 181. See also M. Caulfield, *The Easter Rebellion* (1963), pp. 146–47.

33. *Three Plays*, p. 194.

34. See *1000 Years of Irish Poetry*, intro. Kathleen Hoagland (1947), p. 375.

35. *Drama: The Major Genres*, p. 458.
36. *Three Plays*, p. 204.
37. Ibid., pp. 215–16.
38. Ibid., p. 218.
39. "Sources and Themes," p. 240.
40. *Comedy*, intro. Wylie Sypher (1956), pp. 171–72.
41. "Sean O'Casey and the Road to Expressionism," *Modern Drama*, 4 (1961), 259.

CHAPTER THREE

1. *Inishfallen, Fare Thee Well* (1956), p. 377.
2. *Drums Under the Windows* (1956), p. 331.
3. *Rose and Crown* (1956), p. 134.
4. Letter from O'Casey, Mar. 24, 1960.
5. Letter from O'Casey, July 25, 1959. Joan Templeton points out that O'Casey was introduced to Expressionism with the Drama League's presentation of Ernst Toller's *Masses and Men* (1919) in 1922. See "Sean O'Casey and Expressionism," *Modern Drama*, 14 (1971), 50.
6. *Rose and Crown*, p. 31.
7. Ibid.
8. O'Casey's wife Eileen disclosed that O'Casey habitually hummed when involved in the creative process. Interview with Mrs. O'Casey, Torquay, England, June 13, 1964.
9. *Rose and Crown*, p. 32.
10. Letter from O'Casey, July 25, 1959.
11. R. Hogan, *The Experiments of Sean O'Casey* (1966), p. 188. See also *Blasts and Benedictions*, pp. 99–102.
12. *Rose and Crown*, p. 39.
13. *Three More Plays by Sean O'Casey*, intro. J. C. Trewin (1965), p. xii.
14. Jack Lindsay argues that Heegan, in his parody of the Mass, "is torn like Christ, but meaninglessly, for he cannot recognize the Christ-pattern in his life, in the life of his fellows, and thus move beyond his death to a resurrection into a fuller space of brotherhood and revolt." See *Sean O'Casey: Modern Judgements*, p. 198. Heegan's experiences are somewhat similar to the adventures of John M. Synge's playboy, Christy Mahon, who was also discovered, honored, betrayed, and rejected by the people of Mayo. See H. N. MacLean's "Hero as Playboy," *University of Kansas City Review*, XXI (1954), 9–19. Also, Barney Bagnal is probably patterned after a soldier O'Casey knew, a "Barney Fay, who got field punishment No. 1 for stealin'

poulthry (an Estaminay Cock, maybe) behind the trenches, in the rest camps, out in France?" *Blasts and Benedictions*, p. 100.

15. O'Casey, *Collected Plays*, 2 (1956), p. 7.

16. Ibid., p. 36.

17. Winifred Smith views Susie as a "priestess" who attends the altar in this ironic Graeco-Christian "passion play." "The Dying God in Modern Theatre," *Review of Religion*, V (1941), 267–75. See also Anna Irene Miller, *The Independent Theatre in Europe* (1931), p. 309.

18. See D. Krause, *Sean O'Casey: The Man and his Work* (1966), pp. 157–58 for a discussion of the wine symbolism.

19. M. Malone, *The Plays of Sean O'Casey* (1969), pp. 49–50. See also B. L. Smith's, "From Athlete to Statue: Satire in Sean O'Casey's *The Silver Tassie*," *Arizona Quarterly*, 27 (1971), pp. 347–60.

20. Letter from O'Casey, Mar. 24, 1960.

21. See *Blasts and Benedictions*, p. 101.

22. *The Green Crow*, p. 194.

23. *Rose and Crown*, p. 160. Jack Lindsay contends that the four seasons in the play are "parallel at a religious level to the Canonical Hours of the Breviary." *Sean O'Casey: Modern Judgements*, p. 199.

24. In his discussion of the play in the *Times* (1934), O'Casey stated that the Young Woman was a "symbol of those young women full of life and a fine energy, gracious and kind, to whom life fails to respond, and who are determined to be wicked rather than virtuous out of conformity or fear." "From 'Within the Gates,' " *The New York Times*, Oct. 21, 1934; see also *Blasts and Benedictions*, p. 114.

25. In referring to *Within the Gates* as O'Casey's most comprehensive achievement, G. Wilson Knight argues that the drama is concerned with several ritual struggles. *The Golden Labyrinth* (1962) p. 378.

26. Joan Templeton contends that *Within the Gates* is similar to the "station dramas" as written by some of the German Expressionist dramatists. See "O'Casey and Expressionism," p. 50.

27. *Criticism: the Foundations of Modern Literary Judgement*, p. 270.

28. *The Achievement of T. S. Eliot* (1935), pp. 35–36.

29. O'Casey, *Collected Plays*, 2, p. 119.

30. Sir J. G. Frazer, *The Golden Bough*, one-vol. ed. (1940), pp. 140–41.

31. See *The New Century Classical Handbook*, ed. Catherine B. Avery (1962), pp. 170–74.

32. *The Golden Bough*, p. 141. See also pp. 161–67 for a discussion of Diana and Janus.

33. *Collected Plays*, 2, p. 146.

34. Ibid., p. 147.

35. Ibid., p. 146.
36. Ibid., p. 121.
37. Ibid., p. 222.
38. Ibid., p. 230.
39. Ibid., p. 127.
40. Ibid., p. 133.
41. Ibid., p. 231.
42. Henry Adams uses his two major symbols, the virgin and the dynamo, for similar purposes in *The Education of Henry Adams* (1931). Adams' virgin, like O'Casey's young woman, is associated with centripetal force; Adams' dynamo, like O'Casey's war memorial figure, is associated with centrifugal force. See *The Education*, Chapter XXV.
43. "From 'Within the Gates,' " p. 3.
44. In his commentary on *Purple Dust* O'Casey states that he "abandoned the romantic cult of Nationalism sixty years ago, and saw the real Ireland when I read the cheap edition of Shaw's *John Bull's Other Island.*" *Under a Colored Cap*, p. 263.
45. See S. Cowasjee, *Sean O'Casey: The Man Behind the Plays* (1964) p. 161, and S. J. Ervine, *Bernard Shaw: His Life, Work, and Friends* (1956), p. 372. See also W. C. Daniel's "Patterns of Greek Comedy in *Purple Dust*," *Bulletin of the New York Public Library*, No. 9 (1962), 603–12.
46. *The Genius of the Irish Theatre*, eds. Sylvan Barnet, Morton Berman, and William Burto (1960), p. 31. All subsequent page references will be to this text which was used in the successful Cherry Lane Theatre production in 1956.
47. Ibid., p. 98.
48. Ibid., p. 278. For additional discussion of O'Killigain's function see J. J. McLaughlin's "Political Allegory in O'Casey's *Purple Dust*," *Modern Drama*, 13 (1970), pp. 49–50.
49. Ibid., p. 310.
50. Ibid.
51. For a succinct discussion of Shaw's dramatic technique, see William Irvine's critical introduction to *Bernard Shaw: Selected Plays and Other Writings* (1959), pp. xii–xiii.
52. *The Genius of the Irish Theatre*, pp. 310–11.
53. Ibid., p. 35.
54. Ibid., p. 29. See M. J. Sidnell, "John Bull's Other Island—Yeats and Shaw," *Modern Drama*, 11 (1968), pp. 250–51 for more insight into Doyle's character.
55. Ibid., p. 41.
56. Ibid., p. 94.
57. Ibid., p. 331.

58. See G. W. Knight, *The Golden Labyrinth*, p. 347; see also *Blasts and Benedictions*, p. 66.

59. *The Genius of the Irish Theatre*, p. 82.

60. David Krause has some illuminating comments on the pagan elements in the plays of Synge and O'Casey in " 'The Rageous Ossean' Patron-Hero of Synge and O'Casey," *Modern Drama*, 4 (1961), 284–88.

61. *Under a Colored Cap*, p. 265.

62. Ibid., pp. 266–67. See also *The Experiments of Sean O'Casey*, p. 102.

CHAPTER FOUR

1. J. Campbell, *The Hero with a Thousand Faces* (1967), pp. 3–5, 18–19.

2. *A Collection of Critical Essays* on "The Waste Land," ed. Jay Martin (1968), p. 607; see also *William Faulkner: Three Decades of Criticism*, eds. F. J. Hoffman and O. W. Vickery (1963), pp. 278–79.

3. B. L. Smith, "Satire in O'Casey's *Cock-a-Doodle Dandy*," *Renascence*, 19 (1967), p. 64.

4. J. E. Frazer, *The Scapegoat* (1914) pp. 8–52.

5. *Shakespeare: Modern Essays in Criticism*, ed. L. F. Dean (1957) pp. 176–77, 187.

6. O'Casey, *Collected Plays*, 4 (New York), p. 129.

7. Ibid., p. 132.

8. Ibid., p. 130.

9. Ibid., p. 216.

10. Ibid., p. 217.

11. Ibid., p. 221.

12. *Shakespeare: Modern Essays in Criticism*, p. 83.

13. *Collected Plays*, 4, p. 132.

14. Ibid., p. 146.

15. Ibid., p. 165.

16. Ibid., p. 216.

17. Ibid., p. 214.

18. Ibid., p. 194.

19. Ibid., p. 211.

20. Ibid., p. 217.

21. Ibid., p. 217.

22. Ibid., p. 211.

23. Letter from O'Casey, Oct. 2, 1959.

24. From "O'Casey's Lively Credo," *The New York Times*, Dec. 10, 1958 and reprinted in *Blasts and Benedictions*, p. 144. See also William A. Armstrong, *Sean O'Casey* (1967), p. 30.

25. Reprinted in *Blasts and Benedictions*, p. 141.

26. Father Ned, though viewed by the Establishment as a devilish disrupter of the status quo ("Old Ned," i.e., Satan), is, indeed, a good man in O'Casey's view—a fighter for freedom and joyful creativeness. It is the clergy who dance to a different drummer—if they dance at all. O'Casey had little patience with clerics like Father Domineer, and their plans for programmed obedience to rigid puritanical codes of behavior.

27. *The Sean O'Casey Reader: Plays, Autobiographies, Opinions*, ed. B. Atkinson (1968), p. 532.

28. Ibid., p. 540.

29. Ibid., p. 553.

30. Ibid., p. 557.

31. Ibid., p. 573.

32. Ibid., p. 585.

33. Ibid., p. 591.

34. Ibid., p. 599.

35. See W. V. Spanos, *A Casebook on Existentialism* (1966), p. 173.

Chapter Five

1. Interview with Mrs. O'Casey, Torquay, England, June 13, 1964.

2. See *Twentieth Century Drama: England, Ireland, the United States*, ed. R. Cohn (1966), pp. 168–169.

3. For glimpses of the slum population's conduct during the Easter Week fighting, see M. Caulfield's *The Easter Rebellion* (1946), pp. 196–200.

4. See my "O'Casey, O'Neill, and Expressionism in *The Silver Tassie*," *Bucknell Review*, 10 (1962), pp. 364–69.

5. See P. Esslinger, "*Materia Poetica* of the Two Red Plays," *Modern Drama*, 6 (1963), 53–63.

6. See B. Benstock's *Sean O'Casey* (1970), pp. 49–51.

7. See R. Ayling, "Popular Tradition and Individual Talent in Sean O'Casey's Dublin Trilogy," *Journal of Modern Literature*, 2 (1972), p. 499 for a quick summary of the hostile attitude that O'Casey's plays, especially *The Bishop's Bonfire*, have encountered in Ireland.

SELECT BIBLIOGRAPHY

Armstrong, W. A. *Experimental Drama* (London; G. Bell, 1963). Armstrong sees similarities in the plays of O'Casey and Brendan Behan.

Ayling, Ronald (ed.) *Sean O'Casey: Modern Judgements* (London: Macmillan, 1969). An excellent anthology of critical essays, many of them focusing on O'Casey's late plays.

Benstock, Bernard. *Sean O'Casey* (Lewisburg: Bucknell University Press, 1970).

———(ed.). *James Joyce Quarterly* (Tulsa: the University of Tulsa Press), VIII, Fall, 1970. This is a special O'Casey issue.

Bogard, Travis, and William I. Oliver (eds.), *Modern Drama: Essays in Criticism* (New York: Oxford University Press, 1965).

Carney, James. *Studies in Irish Literature and History* (Dublin: Dublin Institute for Advanced Studies, 1955).

Cowasjee, Saros. *Sean O'Casey: The Man Behind the Plays* (London: Oliver and Boyd, 1963).

Edwards, A. C. (ed.). *Modern Drama* (Lawrence: the University of Kansas Press), IV, Winter, 1961. This issue focuses on the plays of O'Casey and John Millington Synge.

Ellis-Fermor, Una. *The Irish Dramatic Movement* (London: Metheun, 1939).

Hogan, Robert. *The Experiments of Sean O'Casey* (New York: St. Martin's Press, 1960).

Howarth, Herbert. *The Irish Writers, 1880-1940: Literature Under Parnell's Star* (London: Rockliff, 1958).

Koslow, Jules. *The Green and the Red: Sean O'Casey, the Man and His Plays* (New York: Golden Griffin Books, 1950).

Krause, David. *Sean O'Casey: The Man and His Work* (New York: Macmillan, 1960).

Malone, Maureen. *The Plays of Sean O'Casey* (Carbondale: Southern Illinois University Press, 1969).

Mercier, Vivian. *The Irish Comic Tradition* (Oxford: Clarendon Press, 1962).

O'Casey, Eileen. *Sean* (London: Macmillan, 1971).

O'Driscoll, Robert (ed.). *Theatre and Nationalism in Twentieth-Century Ireland* (Toronto: University of Toronto Press, 1971).

Sahal, N. *Sixty Years of Realistic Irish Drama* (Bombay, Macmillan, 1971).

Thompson, William Irwin. *The Imagination of An Insurrection: Dublin, Easter, 1916* (New York: Oxford University Press, 1967).

INDEX

Aaron, 45
Achilles, 49
Agate, J., 42
Angus, 3, 92, 95, 97
Argos, 106
Ariel, 91
Aristotle, 71
Armstrong, W. A., 21, 27, 30, 38
Atkinson, B., 108
Ayling, 15

Bach, J. S., 95
Balashov, P., 9
Barber, C. L., 82
Beckett, T., 54
Bergson, H., 38, 39
Berkeley, G., 1
Bizet, G., 98
Blake, W., 7, 72
Boucicault, D., 65
Brunel, A., 54
Buckstone, J. B., 65
Burns, R., 107
Byron, G., 9

Caesar, J., 72
Caliban, 43
Carroll, S., 54
Cochran, C. B., 42
Cohan, G. M., 89
Coleman, G., 64
Columcille, 97
Conn, 97
Connolly, J., 12
Collins, M., 64
Corkery, D., 65
Crane, S., 56
Cuchulain, 1, 3, 97
Cumberland, R., 65
Curtiss, T., 108

Deasy, J., 5
De Baun, V., 40
Dedalus, S., 46, 98
Defoe, D., 10
Deirdre, 82
De Valera, E., 41, 91
Diana, 59
Dickens, C., 109
Dumbo, 97

Einstein, A., 57
Elistratove, A., 9
Eliot, T. S., 54, 56, 57
Ellmann, R., 10
Emerson, R. W., 44

Fagan, J. B., 42
Falstaff, 82
Frazer, J. G., 59, 80, 81
Frye, N., 85

Goldsmith, O., 8, 44
Gordon, C., 54

Hamlet, 41
Hauptmann, G., 20
Hawthorne, N., 44, 61
Hitchcock, A., 54, 55
Hogan, R., 10, 26, 34

Ibsen, H., 33

Jackson, N., 56
Janus, 58
Jefferson, T., 44
Jesus, 8, 110
John, A., 47
Joyce, J., 2, 24, 25, 56, 63, 68, 90, 98, 99, 105
Jung, C., 80
Juno, 105, 106
Jupiter, 105, 106

Kant, I., 71
Kosciusko, T., 27
Khrushchev, N., 111

Larkin, J., 6, 12, 43, 44, 102, 106
Lear, 41
Lenin, N., 108
Lincoln, A., 23, 44
Locke, J., 71
Lorelei, 82

Mac Diarmada, S., 12
Mammon, 110
Melville, H., 44
McCarthy, J., 88, 89, 102
McGee, D., 100
Matthiessen, F. O., 57
Milton, J., 101
Montague, I., 54
Moore, G., 100
Mozart, W., 95
Murdoch, I., 68

Nathan, G. J., 108
Narcissus, 105
Nichols, B., 42

O'Faolain, S., 65
O'Flaherty, L., 65
Oisin, 49
O'Kelley, S., 65
O'Neill, E., 43, 99, 101, 102, 107
Ophelia, 35
Oscar, 64
Osiris, 80

Parnell, C. S., 43, 106
Peacock, R., 15
Pearse, P., 12, 23, 102
Pinero, A., 42
Plato, 71
Polonius, 35, 36
Pound, E., 24

Shaw, G. B., 2, 3, 4, 5, 6, 8, 43, 44, 65, 67, 68, 70, 76, 100, 101, 108
Schubert, F., 95
Shakespeare, W., 8, 44, 88, 101
Sheridan, R. B., 44, 65
Speight, R., 53
Smith, W., 80
Spinoza, B., 71
Strindberg, A., 47, 93
Sullivan, E., 43, 106, 107
Swift, J., 1, 64, 68

Thor, 8
Tone, W., 21, 29
Thackeray, W. M., 65

Ussher, A., 1, 2, 4, 58

Washington, G., 23
Watts, R., 108
Weston, J., 57
Whitman, W., 44, 46, 111

Yeats, W. B., 2, 6, 10, 29, 41, 46, 65, 79, 99, 100

Zola, E., 20

Sean O'Casey's Drama

was composed in VIP Janson by

Chapman Phototypesetting of Fullerton, California

It was printed and bound by

Lithocrafters, Inc., Chelsea, Michigan.

Project Editor: F. P. Squibb

Book design: Anna F. Jacobs

Production: Paul R. Kennedy